W9-BZD-130

CULTURE SMART!
AUSTRIA

Peter Gieler

·K·U·P·E·R·A·R·D·

First published in Great Britain 2007
by Kuperard, an imprint of Bravo Ltd
59 Hutton Grove, London N12 8DS
Tel: +44 (0) 20 8446 2440   Fax: +44 (0) 20 8446 2441
www.culturesmartguides.com
Inquiries: sales@kuperard.co.uk

Culture Smart! is a registered trademark of Bravo Ltd

Distributed in the United States and Canada
by Random House Distribution Services
1745 Broadway, New York, NY 10019
Tel: +1 (212) 572-2844   Fax: +1 (212) 572-4961
Inquiries: csorders@randomhouse.com

Copyright © 2007 Kuperard

All rights reserved. No part of this publication may be reprinted or
reproduced, stored in a retrieval system, or transmitted in any form or
by any means without prior permission in writing from the Publishers.

Series Editor Geoffrey Chesler
Design Bobby Birchall

ISBN 978 1 85733 347 3

British Library Cataloguing in Publication Data
A CIP catalogue entry for this book is available from the
British Library

Printed in Malaysia

This book is available for special discounts for bulk purchases for
sales promotions or premiums. Special editions, including
personalized covers, excerpts of existing books, and corporate
imprints, can be created in large quantities for special needs.

For more information in the U.S.A. write to Special
Markets/Premium Sales, 1745 Broadway, MD 6–2, New York,
NY 10019 or e-mail specialmarkets@randomhouse.com.

In the United Kingdom contact Kuperard publishers at the
above address.

Cover image: Schönbrunn Palace, Vienna. *Travel Ink/Philip Craven*
Images on pages 13, 14, 16, 17, 35, 60, 66, 70, 85, 93, 106, 113, 116, and 120 by
permission of the Austrian Tourist Office, London.
The print on page 21 is reproduced by permission of Klosterneuburg Abbey.
The photographs on pages 86, 125, 126, and 128 are reproduced by permission
of the author.

CultureSmart!Consulting and **Culture Smart!** guides have both
contributed to and featured regularly in the weekly travel program
"Fast Track" on BBC World TV.

About the Author

PETER GIELER was born in Britain to Austrian parents. After gaining a B.A. in European Studies from the University of Sussex and a Diploma in Educational Technology, he embarked on a long career in educational training for several London authorities, and was Deputy Head Teacher in an Inner London comprehensive school. After retiring, he became General Secretary of the Anglo-Austrian Society. He has published several articles on culture and travel, and is the editor of *Felix Austria*, a quarterly journal about Austria published in the United Kingdom.

Other Books in the Series

- Culture Smart! Argentina
- Culture Smart! Australia
- Culture Smart! Belgium
- Culture Smart! Botswana
- Culture Smart! Brazil
- Culture Smart! Britain
- Culture Smart! Chile
- Culture Smart! China
- Culture Smart! Costa Rica
- Culture Smart! Cuba
- Culture Smart! Czech Republic
- Culture Smart! Denmark
- Culture Smart! Egypt
- Culture Smart! Finland
- Culture Smart! France
- Culture Smart! Germany
- Culture Smart! Greece
- Culture Smart! Guatemala
- Culture Smart! Hong Kong
- Culture Smart! Hungary
- Culture Smart! India
- Culture Smart! Indonesia
- Culture Smart! Ireland
- Culture Smart! Israel
- Culture Smart! Italy
- Culture Smart! Japan
- Culture Smart! Korea
- Culture Smart! Mexico
- Culture Smart! Morocco
- Culture Smart! Netherlands
- Culture Smart! New Zealand
- Culture Smart! Norway
- Culture Smart! Panama
- Culture Smart! Peru
- Culture Smart! Philippines
- Culture Smart! Poland
- Culture Smart! Portugal
- Culture Smart! Russia
- Culture Smart! Singapore
- Culture Smart! South Africa
- Culture Smart! Spain
- Culture Smart! Sweden
- Culture Smart! Switzerland
- Culture Smart! Thailand
- Culture Smart! Turkey
- Culture Smart! Ukraine
- Culture Smart! USA
- Culture Smart! Vietnam

Other titles are in preparation. For more information, contact: info@kuperard.co.uk

The publishers would like to thank **CultureSmart!**Consulting for its help in researching and developing the concept for this series.

CultureSmart!Consulting creates tailor-made seminars and consultancy programs to meet a wide range of corporate, public-sector, and individual needs. Whether delivering courses on multicultural team building in the U.S.A., preparing Chinese engineers for a posting in Europe, training call-center staff in India, or raising the awareness of police forces to the needs of diverse ethnic communities, we provide essential, practical, and powerful skills worldwide to an increasingly international workforce.

For details, visit www.culturesmartconsulting.com

contents

contents

Map of Austria

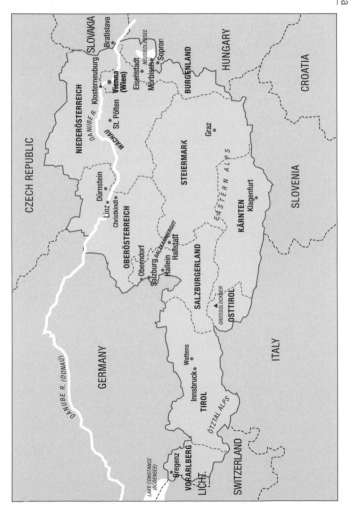

introduction

Today, Austria is a small, neutral country in the heart of Europe. The beauty of its landscape is legendary, drawing visitors in winter for skiing, in summer for mountain and lakeside walking, and all year-round for opera and music. The capital, Vienna, was the jewel in the crown of a cosmopolitan European empire exercising enormous political and intellectual power. The heirs to this glittering past have had a difficult transition to make over the last century.

Defeat in the First World War dramatically reduced Austria's size, removed its monarchy, and left it politically and economically destroyed. The country hardly had time to rebuild and establish a new identity before it became embroiled in another debacle. Again defeated, and now occupied and divided by foreign troops, it started again with the help of the Marshall Plan. The Austrian State Treaty in 1955 was a milestone in the history of the new Republic, setting it on the path to prosperity. The physical damage was repaired, but the traumas of the first half of the twentieth century have certainly left their mark.

Austrians have learned to compromise politically, but they will not compromise their quality of life. They have turned their heritage and culture to good advantage, developed new high-tech industries, and established good relationships with their former Communist neighbors to the east as well as their EU partners. The country has enjoyed a small economic miracle.

Beyond Vienna, there are strong regional differences, and this mixture of different races and traditions has made the Austrians more broad-minded and relaxed than their German-speaking neighbors. They work hard, yet know how to enjoy life. They are hospitable and friendly. They care for their environment and have a strong sense of social responsibility. Boundaries are respected. There are distinct social conventions and expectations that may seem old-fashioned or elaborate by Anglo-American standards, but the young are less conformist in this regard.

Culture Smart! Austria will describe the real people in the picture postcard. It provides an overview of the past, examines their traditions and the values that they live by today, and offers guidelines on what to expect and how to behave in different circumstances. By offering some insights into Austrian life we hope to equip you to discover for yourself the many qualities of this charming, lively, and cultivated people.

Key Facts

Official Name	Republik Österreich	The Republic of Austria is a full member of the European Union.
Capital City	Vienna (Wien)	
Major Cities	Linz, Graz, Salzburg, Innsbruck, Klagenfurt, Bregenz, Eisenstadt, St. Pölten	
Area	32,430 sq. miles (84,000 sq. km)	
Terrain	Mainly Alpine, lowlands in the east	
Climate	Mountain climate, Continental	
Currency	Euro	Austria has been a member of the Eurozone since January 1, 2002.
Population	8,265,900	
Life Expectancy	Males 76.65 Females 82.24	
Ethnic Makeup	German 90.2% Others 9.8%	Other nationalities include Turks, former Yugoslav nationals, and Germans.
Language	German	Slovene- and Croatian-speaking minorities
Religion	Roman Catholic 74% Protestant 4.7% Islamic 4.7% Jewish 4.2% Other 12.4%	Everyone belonging to a recognized Church pays *Kirchensteuer,* or Church tax.

Government	Austria is a democratic federal republic of 8 states (or *Bundesländer*) and Vienna. The seat of government is in Vienna. There are two houses of parliament, the *Nationalrat* and the *Bundesrat*.	The head of state is the President, who is directly elected for 6 years. The head of government is the Chancellor. There are 5 political parties in parliament.
Media	ORF is the national TV and radio network. There are also numerous local stations and commercial satellite stations.	Many national and regional newspapers. Broadsheets: *Die Presse, Der Standard, Wiener Zeitung.* Intermediate format: *Kurier.* Tabloids: *Kronen Zeitung, Kleine Zeitung*
Media: English Language	*Die Presse* and *Austria Today* have Web sites with local and international news.	
Electricity	220 volts, 50 Hz	Two- pronged plugs used. Adaptors needed for US appliances
TV/Video	PAL B system	NTSC TV will not work here.
Telephone	Austria's country code is 43.	To dial out, dial 00. Private companies may have own codes
Time Zone	Central European Time	There is daylight saving in Austria.

chapter one

LAND &
PEOPLE

Austria is a small, landlocked country whose influence has far exceeded its size. The impact of Austrian musicians, artists, and thinkers on European culture has been profound, and its cultural life, even now, draws tourists from far and wide. Its magnificent mountain setting is famous for winter sports. Beautiful in all seasons, and with an enviable quality of life, it is a highly desirable country in which to live and work.

Austria has worked hard to find a role in the modern world. The collapse of Communism in Europe has allowed it once again to engage with the countries of Central and Eastern Europe.

Eight million people live in Austria today. Who are they? What has shaped them, and how do they differ from their German and other neighbors?

GEOGRAPHICAL SNAPSHOT

Austria has a strategic location in the Alps, at the crossroads of Central Europe, with many easily traversable passes and valleys. It covers an area of

32,340 sq. miles (83,871 sq. km), and shares borders with Germany and the Czech Republic to the north, Slovakia and Hungary to the east, Slovenia and Italy to the south, and Liechtenstein and Switzerland to the west. Since 1945 most of its eastern and southern neighbors have suffered from civil unrest, sometimes erupting in revolution. Because of the boundary changes imposed by international agreements, some German-speaking groups found themselves in a minority in another country, for example in South Tyrol (Northern Italy), Czechoslovakia, and Hungary. And Austria today, a German-speaking country, still has minorities of Slovenes and Croats. Vienna and the surrounding regions still enjoy a pan-European attitude to the world, embracing the cultures of former Habsburg lands. If you visit an Austrian town or city today you will hear a multitude of languages, as well as German spoken with many a foreign intonation.

The greater part of Austria is mountainous. Toward the northern and eastern margins the terrain is mostly gently sloping or flat. The magnificent Eastern Alps dominate the landscape of the south and west, with the Grossglockner being the highest point at 12,461 feet (3,798 meters). In both the extreme west and east, Austria shares a lake with one or more of its neighbors: in the west is the Bodensee, or Lake Constance, as it is better known by English-speaking visitors, and in the east is the Neusiedlersee. The former is deep and frequently tempestuous; the latter is shallow and peaceful. Occasionally, as in the winter of 2005–6, the Neusiedlersee freezes over completely and becomes Europe's largest ice rink. It is also a nature reserve and bird sanctuary.

A major feature of the Austrian landscape is its many rivers, most of which flow into the Danube River. The flow from these mountain streams and rivers varies with the seasons, and the level of the Danube rises considerably. During the past three decades much work has been undertaken to control the river and harness its energy by way of hydroelectric power stations and dams. The Danube is a major transport route between eastern and western Europe, now fully open again since the end of the Balkan wars, allowing river traffic to travel freely from the North Sea to the Black Sea.

The Danube is also the setting of some magnificent scenery. The area of the Wachau is renowned for its beautiful castles and ruins, and also for the production of wine. Here is the site of the Nibelungen stories, and also the discovery in 1908 of the Willendorf Venus, an icon of prehistoric art dating from around 24,000 BCE.

The glorious Alpine scenery is a major attraction for tourists. The abundant ski slopes make the west and south a winter sports venue for visitors from all over the world, and the successes of Austrian Alpine skiers in Olympic and World Cup events also play a significant role. Tourism is a major industry in Austria, in both winter and summer seasons. The western areas of the Tyrol and Salzkammergut attract visitors throughout the year. The clever strategic planning of both small and major music festivals also draws tourists at all times.

There is now a
growing debate
among politicians
and the public at
large over the
demands and effects
of tourism and
transportation on

the mountain terrain. There are visible signs of
forest degradation caused by air and soil pollution,
and this issue has become a major topic for
discussion in the European Union.

The historically cold winters, with frequent
snow and rain, coupled with the steep slopes
and poor soil of the Alpine region, have caused a
migration of population to the eastern lowlands.
This is where Austria's industry and wealth are
concentrated, with a distinct emphasis on
development and cooperation with its eastern
and southern neighbors.

A great deal of the countryside remains as
unspoiled woodland, and agriculture is still a
significant part of the economy, with the emphasis
on good quality and organic produce. Austria is
resisting introducing genetically modified crops, and
has the strictest wine laws in the world. However,
modern technology has meant that fewer people are
involved in farming, although most farms are small,
with many diversifying into tourism.

The recent enlargement of the European Union after the fall of the East European Communist regimes has renewed Austrian energy, thus helping it to develop industrial, financial, diplomatic, and cultural links with its neighboring countries, and Vienna is once again becoming an important international center.

CLIMATE

Austria's climate is temperate. The summers are moderate, with occasional showers, and temperatures can be high, with plenty of sunshine. There are cold winters with fog, rain, and snow in the lowlands and snow on the mountains. Very different climatic and weather conditions occur over quite short distances in the deep Alpine valleys. As a visitor, don't take risks: always be sure to seek and follow local advice and opinion, particularly in mountainous regions.

The southeast of the country lies south of the main Alpine ranges and here in the lower valleys and around the lakes the summers may, at times, experience almost Mediterranean heat and dryness. The lakes of southern Austria boast warm water temperatures in the summer months.

THE FÖHN

A warm dry wind known as the *Föhn* usually occurs in Tyrol when a deep layer of prevailing wind is forced over a mountain range. As moist air moves up the windward side, it expands and cools, causing water vapor to precipitate out. The dehydrated air then passes over the crest of the mountain and begins to move down the leeward slope. As it descends to lower levels, the air comes under greater atmospheric pressure and rapidly heats up, creating strong, gusty, warm, dry winds. *Föhn* winds can raise temperatures dramatically in a matter of hours. In the early 1920s the German electrical company AEG registered the trademark "Fön" for its hairdryer, which is a widely used synonym throughout German- and Italian-speaking countries.

These winds are often associated with illnesses ranging from migraines to psychosis. Scientific studies have shown an increase in suicides and accidents during a *Föhn*.

In the east and north the weather can be changeable at all times of the year. The summer months are frequently very hot, but rainfall in this season is more likely to be heavy and thundery, and of short duration.

Temperatures range from 14°F (-10°C) in the mountains and 21°F (-6°C) in the lowlands in winter, although recent experience has shown temperatures much lower than this. Summer temperatures range from 68°F (20°C) in the mountains to 86°F (30°C) in the east and south.

A BRIEF HISTORY

The Alps and the rivers that flowed down the slopes attracted people from the beginning of time. Evidence of settlement of the Danube area in the late Paleolithic Age, some 24,000 years ago, came with the discovery of a small carved stone fertility figure, known to the world as the Venus of Willendorf. In 1991 the sensational discovery of a mummified male body (Ötzi), dating from the Stone Age, was made in the glacial ice of the Ötztal Alps.

Austrian history can be said to start with the Celts. This is a collective term for a multitude of tribes found in central and western Europe during the late Bronze Age (c. 1200 to 700 BCE). They were mainly farmers and cattle breeders who lived in unfortified settlements. We know that there was a vigorous civilization at Hallstatt, in central Austria, where numerous weapons

and ornaments have been found in graves. Over time developments in technology led to the replacement of bronze with iron. The farmers discovered salt, and began to trade with tribes to the south across the Alps, and along river routes to what is now Bavaria. The Celtic kingdom of Noricum was at first a launching pad for attacks on the Roman Empire, then an ally, and was finally incorporated into the Empire in 16 BCE. A museum dedicated to the Celts was opened in 1970 in Hallein.

Gradually the Celts were replaced by Teutonic tribes, and in the second century CE the Roman Emperor Marcus Aurelius marched north to repulse the marauding Germanic hordes, and established Vindobona (Vienna) as a military camp on the Danube to protect the Empire from the northern tribes.

The Babenberg Dynasty
The name "Austria" is first mentioned in a document signed by the Holy Roman Emperor Otto III on November 1, 996, and refers to Ostarrichi, which certifies the donation of the estate "Niuuanhova" (Neuhofen an der Ybbs), *in regione vulgari vocabulo Ostarrichi* ("a region popularly called Ostarrichi"). It appears to have been the name for the territory ruled by the

Babenbergs, which in the eleventh and twelfth centuries became Austria.

The Babenberg family originally came from Bamberg, a town in Upper Franconia on the Main River. Although their ancestry is somewhat vague, by the eleventh century they had become nobles in a number of Bavarian territories. During the 270 years of their rule the Babenbergs managed to create and consolidate the power of the Duchy of Austria. They were skillful rulers, adept at what was later to become a typically Austrian form of aggrandizement, namely the selection of suitable marriage partners from families of equal status. The Duchy grew territorially as the Babenbergs first defended and then expanded their territories from the Bohemians and the Magyars, frequently making advantageous marriages with prominent families from the east and south. This strategy was later emulated by the Habsburg family.

The Babenberg dynasty, often associated with the Germanic saga of the Nibelungen, founded their seat in the Danube basin, creating a powerful fortress at Klosterneuburg. They also established many leading monasteries, such as Melk, Gottweig, and

Heiligenkreuz, as centers of learning and trade. Here the first writings in German were made. This was a time of creative poetic achievement that found expression not only in the Nibelungen saga but also through the music and lyrics of the Minnesingers (courtly minstrels), such as Walter von der Vogelweide.

Duke Leopold V, who had quarreled with him, captured Richard the Lionheart, King of England, on his return from the Third Crusade in 1192 and imprisoned him in the fortress of Dürnstein on the Danube. The huge ransom paid for his release was used to build new frontier fortifications.

Vienna developed into a vibrant trading center under Babenberg rule, and the Danube became an important transport route. The death of the last male ruler, Friedrich II, in 1246 marked the end of the House of Babenberg and their lands were seized by Otakar of Bohemia. Although the country entered a period of great uncertainty, the national identity of an Austrian people had been established. The Austrian character was coming together, molded from a variety of tribes, races, and languages.

The Habsburg Dynasty
In 1278 Otakar himself was defeated at the Battle of Jedenspeigen by Rudolf of Habsburg, and so began

the six-hundred-year reign of this imperial dynasty. The Habsburgs took their name from Habichtsburg Castle, overlooking the Aare River in Switzerland. During the following centuries, by means of clever marriages and treaties but certainly not warfare, the Habsburgs were able to extend their power, dominions, and wealth. They became successive Emperors of the Holy Roman Empire.

THE HOLY ROMAN EMPIRE

The Holy Roman Empire was a loosely federated European political entity that began with the papal coronation of the German king Otto I as the first emperor in 962 and lasted until Francis II's renunciation of the title at the behest of Napoleon in 1806. The Empire was frequently troubled by papal–secular struggles over authority and, after the thirteenth century, by the rising ambitions of nation states. By 1273 the Empire consisted primarily of the Habsburg domains of Austria and Spain, but this included most of Central and Western Europe, excepting France.

In 1519 the young Charles I, Habsburg King of Spain, was crowned Holy Roman Emperor as Charles V at Aachen, and became the most powerful monarch in Europe. His reign was dominated by wars—with France for possession of Italy, and within Germany against the Protestant princes. In 1556 he abdicated and retired to live in a monastery. The Empire was divided between the Habsburg Houses of Austria and Spain. European history owes much to the Habsburgs, and several rulers made significant contributions to European political, religious, philosophical, and cultural development. With the acquisition of new territories, the Habsburgs ruled much of central Europe, including Hungary, Bohemia, and Croatia, parts of Poland, Romania, Bulgaria, Italy, and Ukraine, as well as the Netherlands, Spain, and vast overseas possessions.

In 1571, when the tolerant and cultured Emperor Maximilian II granted his subjects religious freedom, many Austrians turned to Protestantism. However when, in 1576, Emperor Rudolf II embraced the Counter-Reformation, much of the country reverted, with a little coercion, to Catholicism. The attempt to impose Catholicism on the Protestant areas of Europe led to the Thirty Years' War, which started in 1618 and devastated much of Central Europe.

Peace was finally achieved in 1648 with the Treaty of Westphalia. For much of the rest of the century Austria was preoccupied with halting the advance of the Ottoman Empire into Europe. Vienna nearly capitulated to a Turkish siege in 1683, but was rescued by the combined Christian forces of German and Polish–Lithuanian armies. Austrian forces under the command of Prince Eugene of Savoy subsequently swept the Turks to the southeastern edge of Europe.

In 1740, Maria Theresa ascended the throne and ruled for forty years. This period is generally acknowledged as the era in which Austria developed into a modern state. During her reign control was centralized, a civil service was established, the army and economy were reformed, and a system of public education  was introduced. Maria Theresa was the only female ruler of the Habsburg dynasty and together with her son Joseph she established Austria, and especially Vienna, as the musical capital of the world. Joseph's enlightened attitude saw an end to the despotic rule of the Church and censorship.

Progress was halted by events elsewhere in Europe. Revolution broke out in France and Joseph despaired for his sister, Marie Antoinette, its ill-fated Queen. In the harrowing years that followed the Revolution, Napoleon Bonaparte seized control of the French state and embarked upon the conquest of Europe. Austria was overrun by French forces at the battles of Ulm and Austerlitz in 1805. By the terms of the Treaty of Pressburg, certain Austrian territories were ceded to French allies. The treaty marked the end of the Holy Roman Empire, and the last Holy Roman Emperor, Francis II, became instead Francis I, hereditary Emperor of Austria.

The struggle against the French continued, however, and the Tyrolean innkeeper and patriot

Andreas Hofer led a people's rebellion against the joint Franco–Bavarian army occupying Innsbruck to inflict, in August 1809, the first defeat of Napoleon on land. The European conflict continued until Napoleon's final defeat at the battle of Waterloo and the territorial settlement of Europe by the victorious powers— Austria, England, Prussia, and Russia—at the Congress of Vienna in 1815.

Austria, under its brilliant foreign minister Prince von Metternich, dominated the newly created German Federation, which consisted of thirty-nine German states and free cities, and made gains in Italy (acquiring Venetia and recovering Lombardy). These, however, would soon be lost.

Peace did not last long. The seeds of discontent planted by the French throughout Europe erupted in the upheavals of the 1848 revolutions. A combination of forces—the ambitions of a reinvigorated Prussia to lead a united Germany, and the rise of nationalism among the subject peoples of the Habsburg Empire—culminated in the eventual defeat of Austria by Prussia in 1866. This left the Empire mortally wounded and led to the formation of the dual monarchy of Austria–Hungary in 1867 under Emperor Franz Josef I. A period of prosperity followed, but Austria's territories in the Balkans were causing serious problems. International treaties and alliances between the competing powers drove Europe toward disaster, and the assassination of Archduke Franz Ferdinand, the Emperor's nephew and heir to the throne, in Sarajevo in June 1914 by a Serbian nationalist led to Austria–Hungary's declaration of war on Serbia, and ultimately to the First World War.

Franz Joseph reigned longer than any other Habsburg emperor, and died in 1916 at the age of eighty-six. Habsburg rule ended in 1918 with the abdication of Emperor Karl I, who was exiled to Switzerland, and the proclamation of a republic.

The First Austrian Republic

The treaties of Versailles and Saint-Germain left Austria as an impoverished Germanic state with about seven million inhabitants. The dissolution of the Habsburg Empire gave birth to political despair, confusion, and economic disaster. In 1919, Austria's traditional sources of agricultural produce were suddenly and abruptly removed, leading to mass starvation and rising inflation. The newly formed League of Nations arranged a large loan to prevent total economic collapse, but this in turn caused increasing hardship and unemployment.

The internal political situation remained fragile, due to the intense rivalry between Socialist Vienna and the conservative provinces. Austria was in desperate search of a role and function. The differing political groupings were tearing the country apart. Scapegoats were demanded.

Antisemitism had been rife in Austria, and especially in Vienna, during the second half of the nineteenth century. Now, inflamed by the rise to power of Adolf Hitler in Germany and by Nazi propaganda, it resurfaced to become a major and determining feature of interwar politics. The animosity between the Socialists and Conservatives continued to fester and frequent rioting took place. Successive governments dominated by the right-wing Christian Socialist

Party could not quell the unrest or solve the economic problems.

Union between Austria and Germany was forbidden by the treaties of Versailles and St. Germain, but the idea now gained widespread support in Austria. Many Austrians looked north and found their inspiration in the National Socialist Party of Germany, and the rise of Austrian Nazism became a new destabilizing factor at home. Engelbert Dollfuss, the Christian Socialist chancellor, whose party was supported by the Roman Catholic Church, dissolved parliament in 1933 and ruled by decree. He was backed by the Austrian army and his own party militia, the Heimwehr (Home Defense League). Civil war broke out and the government ruthlessly crushed the Socialist opposition.

Dollfuss abolished all political parties except his own, and set about establishing a "truly independent Austrian state." He introduced a new constitution, which dispensed altogether with parliament. In July 1934, Dollfuss was assassinated in an attempted Nazi putsch. The new chancellor, Kurt von Schuschnigg, tried to maintain the status quo, but the government was weakened by internal strife. He attempted to preserve the country from German invasion by trying not to give Hitler an excuse for aggression and cooperating with him as much as possible.

Schuschnigg signed the German–Austrian
Agreement of 1936. This pact recognized the
independence of Austria, but the price was that
Austria's foreign policy had to be consistent with
Germany's. The agreement also allowed Nazis to
hold official posts in Austria. Schuschnigg hoped
that this would appease Hitler. He was wrong.
Hitler demanded that Nazis be given key posts in
the Austrian cabinet. Schuschnigg compromised,
and the Nazi Artur von Seyss-Inquart was made
minister of the interior and security.

The *Anschluss*

Hitler then ordered the Austrian Nazis to create as
much trouble and destruction as possible in order
to put pressure on Schuschnigg. If he could claim
that law and order had broken down, despite the
fact that he himself was responsible for the
breakdown, this would justify marching German
troops into Vienna to restore peace.

Schuschnigg was determined to uphold Austrian
independence, and in the spring of 1938 he called
for a plebiscite. This never took place. At gunpoint
Hitler demanded his resignation, and on March 12
Germany annexed Austria. Adolf Hitler was mobbed
by adoring crowds on his arrival in Vienna. The
First Republic was dead, and Austria was
swallowed up into the expanding German
Reich. A great many Austrians fled their

homeland and traveled to all corners of the world, but thousands were not so fortunate and perished in the concentration camps of the Nazis.

The Second World War

One of the war aims of the Allied Powers (the United States of America, the Union of Soviet Socialist Republics, Great Britain, and France) was the reestablishment of an independent Austria. The wording of the Moscow Declaration of October 1943, that Austria was "a victim" of Nazi Germany, would allow Austrian politicians and the whole establishment to deny any share in responsibility for war crimes for years to come.

In April 1945 Allied troops liberated Austria from Nazi rule, and a provisional government headed by Karl Renner was recognized by the Western occupation powers in October. Elections were held and a coalition government formed.

The Second Austrian Republic and the Allied Occupation, 1945–55

Austria had been divided into four zones of occupation by the Allies. Vienna was similarly divided, but also lay within the U.S.S.R. zone. In 1946, the New Control Agreement gave the Austrian government qualified authority over the entire country, but the occupying powers retained control over such matters as demilitarization and the disposal of German seized property. Subsequent laws eliminated Nazi influence from public life, but former Nazis without criminal records were allowed to participate in general elections in 1949.

The new republic faced huge problems. The country was devastated, and an immediate relief program for social and economic reconstruction was set up with international aid. The economic position slowly recovered. In the very early days of the new government independence became a dominant issue, and Austria's politicians strove to regain full sovereignty from the Allies. After many years of discussions they finally managed to convince the Soviet Union that it had nothing to fear from a free, independent, and neutral Austria. The State Treaty between Austria, France, Great Britain, the U.S.A., and the U.S.S.R. was signed in Moscow in the spring of 1955. All occupying forces were to leave the country by October 1955, and in return Austria had to sign up to a permanent state of political and military neutrality. On May 15, 1955, Chancellor Leopold Figl was able to announce to the crowds gathered outside Schloss Belvedere that "Austria was once again free," and a new future could begin.

Postwar Politics
Consensus politics in the form of coalition governments formed the political scene from 1945

until 1966, and the Social Democratic Party (SPÖ) had been an active member of each government until 2000, when the People's Party (ÖVP) formed a government with the extreme right-wing Freedom Party (FPÖ). The years following the State Treaty saw Austria develop both politically and economically. Prosperity rested in part on the success of the nationalized industries, such as oil, steel, and electricity, and on strict control of the banks. Austria soon became an example of positive industrial relations, where unrest was unheard of. Tourism was fostered and grew rapidly. In 1960 Austria joined the European Free Trade Association and in 1995 became a full member of the E.U.

During the fifty years since the State Treaty Austria has established itself as a country with international responsibilities and an economic force in Central Europe. The collapse of Communism in Europe has enabled it to reopen its traditional markets, and Vienna has once again become the economic leader in the region. Austrian companies and know-how are expanding east and south at a formidable rate.

Controversy has never been far from the political scene, and on at least two occasions has caused international anxiety and alarm. In 1986 Kurt Waldheim, former Secretary General of the

United Nations, was elected President of Austria. It soon came to light that he had lied about his role in the German army during the Second World War. International condemnation aroused indignation and fervent nationalist pride among many Austrians, reflecting their ambivalent attitude to their country's Nazi past.

Again, in 2000, the formation of a government between the center-right People's Party and the far-right Freedom Party, led by Jörg Haider, caused international concern and led to an E.U. boycott of Austria. Haider, an outspoken orator and populist, concentrated on Austrian fears of E.U. enlargement, immigration, and unemployment to gain support. An uneasy relationship between the ruling parties continues, although the SPÖ emerged as the largest party in the 2006 elections.

THE AUSTRIAN PEOPLE TODAY
Today Austria is a small, affluent country whose citizens enjoy a higher standard of living and better quality of life than most of its neighbors. Although unemployment is relatively high, especially in the textile and manufacturing industries, most Austrians are positive about the future. However, there are anxieties about pensions, as recent governments have realized that the current situation is not sustainable. Since the

Second World War Austrians have been able to retire after thirty to forty years' work with thirteen pension payments a year. Therefore, most of the population over the age of fifty-five are retired, still active, and adding additional strains to the economy. It is highly likely that state pensions will be reduced and the retirement age raised.

Austria is a federal country, and each region has its own government and legislature. There is a gulf between the provinces (*Bundesländer*) and Vienna. Since the formation of the republic Vienna has always been much larger and has dominated Austria, and approximately 25 percent of the country's population  lives in the capital. Vienna has never shed its regal past, and indeed recently appears to have rediscovered its imperial role. The opening of cross-country borders and the opportunity for trade with its eastern neighbors has enabled Vienna to welcome visitors and foreign workers alike. In less than forty minutes trains transport travelers and businesspeople to Bratislava in Slovakia and Sopron in Hungary. The airport is expanding, while banking and the insurance industry are opening offices in the new democracies.

Austrians in the provinces are less happy about these advances and are skeptical about the future and the influx of foreign workers. However, tourism is a major source of income and the recent decline in Germany's economic fortunes has caused serious repercussions in certain areas. The summer of 2005 saw the first decline in German tourist numbers for many years.

Austria, once a devoutly Catholic country, is becoming more secular. However, traditions, festivals, and celebrations are very important, and almost every Austrian participates in these in one way or another. Gatherings, whether formal or informal, are essential, and sharing the company of others is a major Austrian characteristic.

AUSTRIAN CITIES

Vienna, the capital of the vast Habsburg Empire, has always been the major focus and most cherished city of all Austrians. The architecture, the town planning, the museums, palaces, concert halls, and opera houses have now made it a world cultural center.

By international standards other Austrian cities are really just large towns, but some of them are jewels. Salzburg, the birthplace of Mozart, is a beautiful baroque city set among magnificent subalpine scenery. This is conservative Austria, with a strong bourgeois ethos, full of high culture and high society.

Innsbruck, huddled and sprawling, is the only city set in the heart of the mountains. An important trading center, it also has significant historical importance.

Further west on the shores of Lake Constance lies Bregenz, the administrative center for the region of Vorarlberg and a busy, thriving city of business and culture.

Graz is the second-largest city in Austria, straddling the Mur River and guarding the entry to the Alps from the south. Often forgotten by tourists, Graz is a comfortable and attractive town set among rolling hills. In the past it often rivaled Vienna, being home to several notable families.

Klagenfurt, a small but interesting provincial town bordering Slovenia, is prosperous and sedate on the shores of Lake Wörthersee.

Linz is the least visited city in Austria, very provincial and predominantly industrial. Here on the banks of the Danube River lie docks alongside chemical- and steel works of international importance.

The town of Eisenstadt, the administrative center of Burgenland, has a population of only 11,000. It is important for being the historical home of the Esterhazy family and their most famous employee, Joseph Haydn. There is also a well-preserved Jewish ghetto there.

AUSTRIA AND THE JEWS

It is impossible to write about Austria without reference to the Austrian Jews. Antisemitism had existed in Europe since the introduction of Christianity. In the early fifteenth century, following the examples of England and Spain, Austria expelled all its Jews. By the reign of Maria Theresa, however, Jews were again to be found in Vienna, having arrived from Russia and Poland or with the Ottoman invaders from the south and east. Maria Theresa banished the Jews from Vienna and the neighboring territories, but her son Joseph partly repealed the ban and allowed them to settle in the towns surrounding the capital. One can find the remains of many Jewish communities and cemeteries in towns on a radius of thirty to fifty miles (50 to 80 km) from Vienna.

Following the revolutions of 1848, Franz Joseph made many internal reforms and granted Jews the right to enter and live in Vienna. By the beginning of the twentieth century more than 185,000 Jews had settled in the capital. The proportion of Jewish students at the university far exceeded that of the indigenous population, and

Vienna had more Jewish teachers, lawyers, and doctors per head than any other city in Europe.

The late nineteenth century also saw the rise of modern mass antisemitism. Jews were frequently attacked by Viennese mobs, encouraged by several politicians, including the Christian Social mayor of Vienna, Karl Lueger. Then hardship and economic depression followed the First World War and enabled Austrian nationalists to create a convenient scapegoat; they were assisted by leading politicians and, of course, the Nazis.

Kristallnacht

After the *Anschluss* life became increasingly difficult for the Jews, but the early hours of November 10, 1938, brought crisis. Following the assassination of a German diplomat in Paris by a Polish-Jewish youth, Joseph Goebbels, Hitler's minister for propaganda and national enlightenment, orchestrated a pogrom against all Jews in the Third Reich. A night of violent action by storm troopers, the SS, and the Hitler Youth resulted in death or injury for hundreds of Jews, massive destruction of their property and businesses, and the gutting of synagogues. (The name *Kristallnacht*, given to this night, is a reference to the broken glass resulting from the destruction.) Those Jews who could, escaped. Those who remained suffered further persecution, until their final deportation to the killing grounds and concentration camps of central and eastern Europe. Many Austrian Jews who had made notable contributions to the country fled or were killed. An estimated 65,000 Austrian Jews, out of a prewar population of 80,000, perished in the Holocaust.

It took until the late 1990s for Chancellor Franz Vranitzky to voice public acceptance of and an apology for Austrian culpability in the crimes committed against its Jews. Remarkably, many Viennese survivors of the Holocaust maintain a positive affection for their home city. In spite of the suffering and loss, many return, if not to stay, then frequently to visit the city of their birth.

Austria's, and especially Vienna's, Jewish inheritance is highly significant. Jews made huge contributions to its scientific, medical, and legal life, as well as to theater, art, music, and publishing.

GOVERNMENT TODAY

Austria is a federal republic consisting of nine states, or *Bundesländer* (singular, *Bundesland*).

The constitution was established in 1922 and revised in 1929. The head of state, the president, is elected directly by popular vote for a six-year term. The Federal Assembly consists of the National Council, or Nationalrat (183 members elected by direct popular vote to serve a four-year term) and the Federal Council, or Bundesrat (sixty-two members representing the *Bundesländer* on the basis of population, but with each state having at least three representatives, serving a five- or six-year term).

State	Capital
Burgenland	Eisenstadt
Carinthia (Kärnten)	Klagenfurt
Lower Austria (Niederösterreich)	St. Pölten
Upper Austria (Oberösterreich)	Linz
Salzburg (Salzburgerland)	Salzburg
Styria (Steiermark)	Graz
Tyrol (Tirol)	Innsbruck
Vorarlberg	Bregenz
Vienna (Wien)	Vienna (Wien)

Austria is a multiparty democracy. If a party can win 5 percent of the vote in an election it is entitled to a seat in the Nationalrat. The main political parties are shown below.

ÖVP: The Austrian People's Party (right of center) is roughly comparable to the German Christian Democratic Union in terms of both platform and voter demographics. The People's Party was founded immediately following the reestablishment of the Federal Republic of Austria in 1945, and has been a major player in Austrian politics ever since.

SPÖ: The Social Democratic Party of Austria (left of center) is one of the oldest political parties in Austria. The SPÖ is one of the major parties in the country and has particularly strong ties to labor unions and the Austrian Chamber of Labor (Arbeiterkammer).

Die Grünen: The Austrian Green Party (left-wing) was formed in 1986. Apart from ecological issues such as environmental protection, the Greens also campaign for the rights of minorities and advocate a socio-ecological (*ökosozial*) tax reform. Their basic beliefs are "direct democracy, non-violence, ecology, solidarity, feminism, and self-determination." The majority of the issues that the Greens champion cater to an especially young, urban, and more highly educated class of voters.

FPÖ: The Austrian Freedom Party (extreme far-right) is formerly associated with the name of Jörg Haider, who is no longer a party member. Its current leader is Heinz-Christian Strache. The FPÖ is generally regarded as a populist party and often classed as a Euronationalist party. It promises stronger anti-immigration laws, stricter law enforcement, and more funds for families. In April 2005, Jörg Haider and other leading party members seceded from the FPÖ to form a new party, the Alliance for the Future of Austria.

BZÖ: The Alliance for the Future of Austria

(far right) was founded on April 4, 2005, by Jörg Haider, his sister Ursula Haubner, and other leading members of the Freedom Party of Austria (FPÖ). This resulted in the split of the Freedom Party, the future prospects of which seemed very uncertain for a time. In recent state elections, however, the BZÖ fared very badly, and since then the party has retreated to Haider's original base in Carinthia.

KPÖ: The Communist Party of Austria

was established in 1918. Banned between 1933 and 1945, it played an important role in the Austrian resistance against the Nazis and fascism. The party publishes a newspaper called *Volksstimmen* (previously *Volksstimme*) and runs in elections. However, it has not had representation in the federal parliament since 1959. It went on to receive an exceptional 20 percent of the vote in the 2003 Graz local elections, and in 2005 it returned to its first state parliament in thirty-five years after winning 6.3 percent of the vote in Styria.

CONSENSUS POLITICS AND THE ECONOMY

Since 1945 consensus politics has played a major role in the economic recovery and stability of Austria. The country has been governed mainly by coalition governments and the tradition of mediation and compromise continues into the twenty-first century.

This has enabled Austria to establish a well-developed market economy with a high standard of living. With exports of goods and services reaching more than 40 percent of GDP, Austria's economy is closely integrated with other E.U. member countries, especially with Germany. Austria's entry into the E.U. has drawn an influx of foreign investors attracted by its access to the single European market.

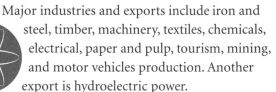

Major industries and exports include iron and steel, timber, machinery, textiles, chemicals, electrical, paper and pulp, tourism, mining, and motor vehicles production. Another export is hydroelectric power.

A far cry from the days immediately after the end of the First World War, Austria is now self-sufficient in agricultural products, boasting one of the largest organic industries in Europe.

The Eurozone

As a fervent member of the European Union and the Eurozone, Austria has now adopted the euro in place of the Austrian schilling.

Austria is at the center of industrial development and influence in Central Europe, and is investing heavily in the former Communist countries. It relishes its new role and is actively promoting Vienna as a center for international business and achievement, where the United Nations and OPEC are already firmly established. To meet competition from the Central European countries, especially the new members, Austria is emphasizing knowledge-based sectors of the economy. The aging population, together with high health and pensions costs, poses some serious problems for future tax and welfare policies.

Austria has a major role to play in the heart of Europe, drawing on its past experience. Its active contribution to the cultural development of modern Europe is significant. The Austrian tradition of compromise in negotiations, whether political, social, economic, or cultural, is a potential model for Europe and beyond.

chapter two

VALUES & ATTITUDES

The Austrians are very different from their German neighbors. More broad-minded and relaxed, they have been molded by a different history and by the close proximity of many other nations. This is, however, still a well-organized and very tidy country. The Austrians are aware that an ordered society requires rules, and this is something they value and appreciate.

TOWARD A NEW IDENTITY

Austria today consists only of the German-speaking regions of its former empire. Not wishing to be seen as the poor relations of Germany, the Austrians spent most of the twentieth century searching for a new identity. Even today people see themselves primarily not as Austrian but as a native of their region, as Carinthian, Styrian, or Tyrolean. After the First World War, however, the people of Salzburg expressed a wish to become part of Germany, and after the Second World War those of the Vorarlberg wanted to join Switzerland.

Since joining the European Union, most Austrians have been content to be Austrian, and their confidence has grown after the collapse of Communism in Eastern Europe. Relations with former provinces and neighboring nations have never been so positive. The business and social interchange with Slovaks, Czechs, Hungarians, and Croatians grows daily. Vienna has been totally refurbished, its splendid buildings restored to their former glory, and the business community is once again the center of activity in Central Europe. The recent celebration of fifty years of the State Treaty has become a watershed, and Austria is firmly looking to the future.

As a result of the recent influx of peoples, Austrians once again live in a multicultural society, and are exposed to diverse traditions. However, local patriotism is strong in rural areas; in Carinthia, for example, a notorious chauvinism is sometimes evident that is not unconnected with the presence of a sizable Slovene minority. Austrians may argue vociferously against immigration from the erstwhile Eastern Bloc while being eager and happy to employ "illegal" care workers to look after the old and infirm.

Patriotism
The Austrians have a great love for their *Heimat*, or region. This love is often not fully realized or appreciated until they are abroad. Then even the

mention of Mannerschnitten (Viennese hazelnut wafers) or Almdudler (a soft drink) will bring tears of nostalgia to the eye. The sound of Viennese music or an Alpine folk song can reduce them to quivering wrecks.

The typical Austrian is a complex character, giving the immediate appearance of laid-back conviviality (*Gemütlichkeit*) and friendly hospitality. He is charming, well able to mediate and compromise, and generally honest. He is well educated, can hold forth on diverse topics of conversation with a good sense of humor, and has style. However, beneath this urbane veneer lies a frustration and resentment that now and again rises to the surface. Many Austrians are unable to rid themselves of a deep xenophobia. This may well stem from feelings of superiority inherited from their imperial past, and a justifiable pride in the pan-Germanic cultural achievement.

Coming to Terms With the Past
Austrians took much longer than their German neighbors to admit any culpability for their actions in the Second World War. History books still have large gaps for the years 1933–45. Austrian politicians and bureaucrats took refuge behind the 1945 Potsdam Agreement, in which the the Allies declared that Austria was the first victim of Nazi Germany. The truth was far from

this. Hitler was welcomed with open arms. Most Austrians were eager supporters of the aims of the Third Reich, and many were members of the Nazi Party. There was no general denazification program in Austria after the war, and many civil servants and politicians merely changed their coats. It took five decades for the Republic to apologize officially to the victims of the Nazis.

Recently there have been increased efforts by Austrians to atone for the past. Schools invite survivors to come and talk to pupils, and in 2003 there was a campaign called "Letter to the Stars" for all schools in Austria to "adopt" and research the fate of a Holocaust victim. This culminated in a gathering of 15,000 schoolchildren and students in Vienna and the publication of a book.

A number of towns are officially recognizing the contributions made by victims of the Holocaust, and in another project, "Stolpersteine," small commemorative bronze plaques are set in the paving stones outside the last dwelling-places of the Jews. This action has been greatly appreciated by the victims' relatives, for whom it is a form of acknowledgement and acceptance after many years.

QUALITY OF LIFE

The Austrians have an enviably high quality of life, and they know when they are well-off. They live in a beautiful country, and they care deeply about their environment, going to some lengths to protect it. The cost of living is not as high as in many other European countries, and it is generally possible to have a comfortable life. They enjoy generous holiday allowances, and have achieved a happy work–life balance. Austrians eat and drink well, and take a considerable amount of exercise. They revel in the outdoor life, and often walk or cycle for hours in the mountains or countryside, ending up in a good country restaurant or lakeside tavern.

Elegant modern housing, a good car, good clothes, and good food all indicate status. Being able to build one's own house, for example, even if it takes years, is enormously important.

CONFORMITY AND CRITICISM

However strong their fears or frustrations may be about political and social change, Austrians conform. People will criticize authority, but still accept it—in the home, school, workplace, and local and national government. Austrians prefer the familiar, the tried and tested, to novelty. They are naturally conservative, with deeply held beliefs and traditions, but as materialism encroaches some of these are becoming hollow, and may not survive except, perhaps, for the purposes of tourism.

Criticism features large in everyday Austrian life. People will complain and argue about conditions and every new ruling, and rail to friends and family against the ridiculous laws of the European Union, the country's lax immigration rules, and the rise in organized crime—but that is as far as it goes. The sole form of rebellion appears to take place behind the wheel of a car, where these normally docile Europeans turn into reckless monsters.

Critical Thinking
Despite their reluctance to rock the boat, the Austrians have a strong tradition of critical intellectual thought. They enjoy satire and the undermining of authority, and often express this through literature. There was strict censorship in Vienna until 1848, and it fell to playwrights and poets to challenge the rules and regulations. Johann Nestroy and Franz Grillparzer wrote and performed in plays highly critical of society, with veiled attacks against the censor. In the final days of the Habsburg Empire writers such as Karl Kraus and Arthur Schnitzler openly questioned the values of society and the teachings of the Church, and were critical of both the government and public opinion.

During the early part of the twentieth century Vienna became a home of radicalism and of groundbreaking advances in psychology. Lenin and Trotsky spent time in Vienna. Freud, Jung, and Adler met in coffeehouses and taught at the University. Postwar thinkers and writers such as Thomas Bernhard, Ingeborg Bachmann, and Elfriede Jelinek continued the Austrian tradition of questioning received values and opinions.

Curiously, many Austrian poets and dramatists managed to combine their creative and critical writing careers with a safe job in the state sector, within the system. Franz Grillparzer, Austria's most famous playwright, remarked that his countrymen "held greatness to be dangerous and fame an empty vanity."

ATTITUDES TO NEIGHBORS

Austria is surrounded by many countries, some of which are former territories of the Habsburg Empire. In the past there was conflict with many of these neighbors; for example, for large periods of time a state of war existed between Bavaria and Austria. Also, the Empire embraced a vast geographical area and tensions existed within and between its many peoples. Today Austria's relationships with its neighbors are positive, although in the 1950s and '60s there was tension and debate with Italy over the erosion of the guaranteed regional autonomy of the South Tyrol

(Alto Adige), the German-speaking northern province ceded to Italy after the First World War, and over its right to retain its own wealth; and also more recently with the Czech Republic regarding the stability of the Temelin, a nuclear power station very close to the Austrian border.

Austrians have always regarded themselves as the champions and protectors of German culture, citing the succession of artists, writers, and composers who lived and worked in Vienna and the surrounding area, and looked down on their neighbors as mere peasants by comparison. Today they relish their success in winter sports, and especially their superiority over Swiss, German, and Italian skiers. Their attitude to Germany might be described as a feeling of cultural superiority tinged with envy. German television and other media dominate Austria, and this certainly colors the relationship between the two countries.

The tensions and differences of the past, however, are diminishing with the rise of a more relaxed and cosmopolitan younger generation, who are more flexible and who see similar problems and difficulties throughout Europe.

STATUS
The Austrian love of stability and conformity often takes the form of nostalgia for the social

hierarchy of the Habsburg Empire, where every rung on the ladder was clearly defined. Austrian society is obsessed with titles and forms of address that perform the functions of boosting your own status and of flattering the people who, you hope, will advance your interests. Visitors to Austria ignore the importance of titles at their peril. Even a captain of industry will need a title to be taken seriously.

Titles are commonly used in every sphere of society. A bachelor's degree entitles you to present yourself, for example on the nameplate by your front door, as, say, Frau or Herr Magister Smith or, in the case of a qualified engineer, as Diplom-Ingenieur Black. Even a builder or baker is Herr Meister. A title helps when you want to make a restaurant reservation or hotel booking, and will be a significant advantage if you are trying to secure a special theater or opera ticket.

ATTITUDES TO WEALTH AND SUCCESS

Austria is one of the wealthier countries of Europe, and individual Austrians are proud of their positions and possessions. Attitudes to money and success are, at best, ambivalent. There is a great deal of envy and "keeping up with the Schmidts." Someone who refurnishes their house or purchases a new car will be eagerly interrogated with questions such as, "How much did it cost?" "What discount did you get?" Really, however, the questioner will want to know, "Where did you get the money?"

Despite the obsession with rank and titles, Austria is, broadly speaking, a meritocracy; but people are skeptical of success. "*Wer steht dahinter?*" ("Who is behind him?") is a question commonly asked, often not unreasonably, for certain jobs within both the state and the private sectors are open to political patronage. Membership in a political party may well be a stepping-stone to promotion. Civil servants may become politicians, and vice versa, and occasionally this blurring of roles has led to intrigue and corruption.

PRUDENCE

The Austrians have become fanatical savers. Everyone has a *Sparbuch* (deposit or savings account), although these often pay a pitiful rate of interest. Although E.U. regulations are changing the administration of this form of saving, it is still central to the Austrian way of life. People work conscientiously, and the rewards are safely put away. They remember the past and the economic disasters of the early twentieth century, and are pessimists about the future—things could get worse, so something

must be put by for an emergency. That
emergency may well strike on retirement, as the
country begins to realize that it can no longer
afford the generous pensions of the past.

DUTY

Doing one's duty is an important part of life, but
not as strictly enforced as it is in Germany. For
example, a notice in a German park would state,
"Walking on the grass is strongly prohibited,"
whereas in Austria such a sign would say, "Please
keep off the grass." There is a sense of communal
responsibility, seen in the cleaning of public
passages and staircases in apartment blocks, and
sweeping leaves and snow from the front of the
building. "Do to others as you would have them
do to you" is applied; therefore don't mow your
lawn or repair your car on Saturday afternoon or
Sunday, so as not to disturb your neighbors.

THE WORK ETHIC

The Austrians work hard. They are reliable and
efficient. They start early—often earlier than their
official starting time—and they finish early. They
do what is expected of them, and what they have
contractually agreed to do, and waste as little time
as possible. It is rare to see anyone working late,

putting in extra hours, or taking work home. This would be seen as a sign of personal inefficiency.

PRIVATE AND PUBLIC

Boundaries are important and clearly defined. The Austrians appreciate their homes and their time off, but these are private matters, and never discussed at work. Equally, work and its problems are hardly ever discussed at home, and work colleagues generally remain just that. If colleagues do meet socially, they don't talk about their work. Bosses and workers don't socialize.

Work and Play Don't Mix

One evening the director of a major scientific research organization in Vienna was persuaded by his daughter to go with her to hear a popular modern jazz group. When they arrived and sat down at a table near the stage, the band was already playing. The director was surprised and disconcerted to be confronted by the head of his research department on the lead guitar. He'd had no inkling of his employee's other life, and on later investigation discovered that in his youth he had played in a heavy rock group that had made several recordings. This chance meeting was a social embarrassment for both men, and was never mentioned later in the office.

chapter three

CUSTOMS & TRADITIONS

It is heartening and somewhat surprising to find so many local traditions still thriving throughout Austria. The mixture of ancient pagan rites and celebrations with deeply Christian religious festivals brings an abundance of color and vibrancy to many villages and towns. Tradition is very important, with each region of Austria maintaining its own identity not only in the form of dialect but also of national costume. Women wear the *Dirndl*, which has a tight bodice, low neck, full skirt, lacy blouse, and apron, mainly for special occasions, but in some country areas it is the dress of every working day. Music is an essential part of the local scene, and each village boasts a brass band, which happily supports local festivities, celebrations, weddings, and even funerals.

RELIGION

There is no state religion in Austria, but some 88 percent of Austrians are officially Christian, of whom 78 percent are Roman Catholic. The increase in the number of people apparently without religious affiliation may have come about because recognized religious organizations in Austria are financed by a state tax on their members, the so-called *Kirchensteuer* (Church tax), which amounts to approximately 1 percent of their income. Many people who do not want to pay this tax officially withdraw from their religious communities.

In 1867, when the Austro–Hungarian Empire instituted freedom of religion for all religious groups, these included Catholics, Protestants, Greek Orthodox, and Jews.

In 1908 the Empire annexed Bosnia Herzegovina, a country with a significant number of Muslims. In 1912 it became the first state in Europe to recognize Muslims as a religious minority. In recent years, an influx of foreign workers and refugees from Turkey and the former Yugoslavia has increased the percentage of Muslims living and practicing their religion in Austria.

Today, Methodists, Mormons, and Buddhists are recognized religious minorities in Austria.

Before the Second World War, about 250,000 Jews lived in Austria. Today, the Jewish community has about 7,000 members, mostly recent immigrants from the former Soviet Union.

The Influence of the Church

Austria is a profoundly Roman Catholic country. Historically, the Emperor, as head of the Holy Roman Empire, was viewed as the secular protector of the Church, and was at the forefront of the Counter-Reformation; during the sixteenth, seventeenth, and eighteenth centuries, the state took a public stand against all non-Catholics.

There are many religious festivals throughout the year that have been adopted as national holidays.

Here traditional religious processions and ceremonies frequently involve entire communities. On days such as Corpus Christi or the Assumption of Mary, Church and village celebrate together with festivals of flag-waving and brass bands as well as sung mass and colorful processions.

Recently the effects of globalization and internationalism have led to a decline in church attendance and to a crisis in the Church in Austria. There are very few men entering the priesthood, and the Church is now reliant on priests from other countries. Most Austrians still attend mass on special occasions such as Christmas Eve, however.

Austria abounds in monasteries, many of which play an important role in education.

MARIAZELL

The most important pilgrimage site in Austria is the basilica of Mariazell, in the north Styrian Alps, a hundred miles (143 km) north of Graz. The church contains a miraculous image of the Virgin Mary, carved in lime-wood, which was given in 1157 and draws pilgrims from all over Central Europe.

In 2005 the Catholic Church chose Mariazell as the venue for a Central European pilgrimage. Just before the prescribed day, however, the weather broke. It rained incessantly, lasting through the day itself, and emergency plans had to be carried out. The organization was a model of efficiency. The large areas that had been allocated for parking were sodden, so they were closed, and the thousands of buses coming into Mariazell were directed to park on the approaching roads. The 250,000 pilgrims walked in pouring rain for miles; those inadequately dressed were given waterproof clothing; all were given food and drink; and, amazingly, fewer than ten people missed their return bus. (After the festival the organizers were amazed that the pilgrims had correctly sorted all their litter for recycling!)

This pilgrimage will be repeated in 2007, when the Pope will visit Mariazell and celebrate mass for the 850th anniversary of the basilica.

NATIONAL AND RELIGIOUS FESTIVALS

National festivals are standard throughout the country, and include all the major religious celebrations.

DATE	FESTIVAL	ENGLISH NAME
January 1	*Neujahrstag*	New Year's Day
January 6	*Dreikönigstag*	Epiphany
March/April	*Palmsonntag*	Palm Sunday
March/April	*Ostersonntag*	Easter Sunday
March/April	*Ostermontag*	Easter Monday
May 1	*Tag der Arbeit*	Labor Day/May Day
May/June	*Christi Himmelfahrtstag*	Ascension Day
May/June	*Pfingstsonntag*	Whit Sunday
May/June	*Pfingstmontag*	Whit Monday
May/June	*Fronleichnam*	Corpus Christi
August 15	*Mariä Himmelfahrt*	Assumption Day
October 26	*Nationalfeiertag*	National Holiday
November 1	*Allerheiligen*	All Saints' Day
December 8	*Maria Empfängnis*	Conception of Mary
December 25	*Weihnachtsfeiertag*	Christmas Day
December 26	*Weihnachtsfeiertag (2)*	Boxing Day

Christmas

Christmas is, of course, an important religious and family festival in Austria. During Advent, the four weeks before Christmas Day, markets appear in town and village centers selling all sorts of traditional goods such as wooden table and tree decorations, mulled wine (*Glühwein*), and seasonal delicacies, while local choirs and brass bands entertain the crowds with Christmas carols. These markets have become major tourist attractions, and many busloads of visitors travel from some distance to participate in the festivities.

Stille Nacht, Heilige Nacht

The best-loved Christmas carol of all comes from Austria. On Christmas Eve, 1818, the assistant priest at the parish of St. Nicholas in Oberndorf, near Salzburg, Joseph Mohr, handed over a poem to the organist and local schoolteacher, Franz Gruber, and asked him to write a fitting melody for two solo voices, a choir, and guitar accompaniment. Coming from this simple beginning, Mohr and Gruber gave the world "Silent Night."

The carol met with general approval at its first performance, then the following Christmas, 1819, the original Rainer Family Singers reportedly sang it in the parish church of Fügen, in Zillertal. Three years later, in 1822, they perfomed it at Bubenberg Castle on the occasion of a visit by Emperor Franz I of Austria and Tsar Alexander I of Russia. After that it became established as a firm favorite, known and loved all over the world. Special services are held at the small church in Oberndorf each year.

In Oberösterreich the small village of Christkindl (which means "Infant Jesus") plays host to a special festive post office each year during Advent. Children from all over Austria write to "Christkindl" with their Christmas wishes, and each child receives a response in an envelope with a commemorative stamp and franked with a special Christmas postmark. These envelopes are eagerly collected by philatelists throughout the world.

During the Advent period there is another tradition that finds its roots in pagan times. St. Nikolaus Day, December 6, is a feast day for children in many parts of the world. The evening before St. Nikolaus, however, belongs to Krampus. This person is an alarming sight—almost the devil himself. He has horns, and from his hideous mouth droops a long, slobbering tongue. He wears clothes of bright red and black. He traditionally carries a basket on his back in which to carry unruly children off to hell, but more recently he has abandoned his basket as being too terrifying for children. Krampus still drags his clanking chain with him, rattling and shaking the ground. As he passes, dogs howl and cats spit in terror. He also carries a birch rod, and this associates him with Ruprecht, the follower and companion of St. Nikolaus. The origins of Krampus are unclear, but he is a genuine Austrian phenomenon.

St. Nikolaus, on the contrary, who appears in his bishop's robes and brings gifts to children, is certainly not Austrian. He was bishop of Myra in Asia Minor at the start of the fourth century, and there are two well-known legends associated with him. The first concerned a poor father who could not raise the dowry for his three daughters, and the second is the story of three children who had been cruelly murdered and were restored to life by the saint. How Krampus and Nikolo, as he became known, got together is not known. The former punished the naughty, and the saint rewarded the good and dutiful.

Christmas family celebrations take place on December 24. Shops, offices, and transportation systems close down around midday. Presents are exchanged, brought by the "Christkindl" in the early evening (*Die Bescherung*), and a light meal, usually carp, is eaten. Traditionally families then attend midnight mass.

Christmas Day is a much quieter affair, spent visiting friends or going skiing. The traditional Christmas fare of goose is now giving way to turkey and *Wiener Schnitzel*.

Silvester and New Year's Day
New Year's Eve (Silvester) is a huge and noisy celebration. Lucky charms are exchanged, mostly

in the form of marzipan pigs. There are a few
other traditions, such as dropping pieces of
molten lead into water and telling fortunes from
the resulting shapes. Just before midnight people
take to the streets with bottles of champagne or
Sekt and at the stroke of midnight the pealing
bells of St. Stephan's Cathedral in Vienna are

broadcast over
loudspeakers, followed
immediately by the
"Blue Danube" waltz.
Austrians waltz around
the town squares
shouting "*Prosit
Neujahr!*"

January 1 is usually spent quietly with the
family. Most Austrians watch the famous New
Year's Day Concert from Vienna on the huge
open-air screen or on television. The audience is
quite critical of each concert, comparing the
present offering to those in the past.

Epiphany
Just before the schools reopen there is the feast of
Heilige Drei Könige (Three Wise Men). Children
dress up and go from door to door collecting
sweets. Above many doors are chalked the letters
of "C+M+B," and the date. These initials stand for
the names of the three Kings (Caspar, Melchior,

and Balthasar), and denote a blessing on the house for the coming year.

Another old pagan custom originating in the Salzburg and Tyrol regions is *Perchten*. Originally, this word referred to the female masks representing the entourage of Frau Bercht, an ancient goddess. Traditionally, the masks were displayed in processions during the last week of December and first week of January, and particularly on January 6. There is now a movement to display the *Perchten* in their true and original form, and a number of societies have been established to produce authentic customs, dances, and stories. Little children watch spellbound as these huge and horrific monsters dance and mill around them, shouting and hooting, with cowbells attached to their waists.

Easter

Religious observances leading up to this most important festival of the Christian year start with a service on Palm Sunday at which *Palmkätzchen* (branches of pussy willow) are blessed, taking the place of palms. Holy Week is kept in traditional Roman Catholic fashion, with prayers at the seven

Stations of the Cross, and culminates in the Easter vigil on the Saturday night, leading to the first and most special mass of Easter Day. (Good Friday is an ordinary working day, and there is no special Good Friday service except for the Stations of the Cross.)

Most houses, as well as shop windows, are decorated with branches of pussy willow, Easter eggs, and the *Osterhase* (Easter Bunny). The *Osterhase* decorates hard-boiled eggs (traditional Easter eggs in Austria are not made of chocolate) and hides them in the garden for the children to find. Dining tables are decorated with pussy willow, spring flowers, and more beautifully hand-painted eggs. Easter is a family time—short, as there are no school holidays, but enjoyable none the less. *Fochaz* (Easter bread) is braided and baked for the Easter feast.

Easter fires burn on Alpine mountain peaks after sunset on Easter Saturday, and small bands of musicians walk through the towns, playing hymns and other traditional tunes. These fires are sometimes called Judas fires, because effigies of Judas Iscariot were frequently burned in them. The Easter eve bonfires predate Christianity, however, and were originally intended to celebrate the arrival of spring. The burning of an effigy symbolized the victory of spring over winter.

In Vienna and Salzburg, there are Easter concerts featuring classical music.

Other Religious Festivals

The feast of Corpus Christi dates back to the twelfth century. The first recorded Corpus Christi procession was held in 1623 in Hallstatt, situated at the foot of the Dachstein Mountain and restricted to a small territory by the lake. The significance of Hallstatt's procession is that it is also held on large floating barges on the lake—a reminder of the time when salt from the mines was transported by water. The ceremony begins with high mass in the pilgrimage and parish church of Our Dear Lady of the Mountain, after which the procession makes its way to the four stations to be blessed. The ceremony ends with final blessings given in the church and the singing of a ceremonial hymn.

Again on August 15, for the Feast of the Assumption of Mary, there are processions, and altars are erected and decorated out of doors.

NONRELIGIOUS FESTIVALS AND EVENTS

Many other traditional Austrian events have nothing to do with religion. Local festivals include *Kirtag*, a village fair, and *Schützenfest*, one that incorporates a shooting competition, and many

beer, wine, and flower festivals. In some areas
villages have their own local festivals, and there
are many local productions of plays and operettas.

Major international festivals, such as the
Vienna Music Festival in the spring and the
renowned summer music festivals in Salzburg,
Bregenz, and Mörbisch, are very popular. There
are also firework displays along the Danube River.

The burning of effigies at the end of a season is
popular in country areas, especially around
Midsummer's day, June 21, and, as we have seen,
at the end of winter. There are also traditions such
as the decorating of the May Tree on May 1 and
the more unusual celebration of *Dachgleiche*, or
topping-out ceremony, when the shell of a
building has been completed. This is done by
attaching a small tree to the top of the building.
The workers are thanked with food and a crate or
two of beer.

On the first day of *Volkschule* (primary school), small children receive a *Schultüte*. As in Germany, this is a cardboard cone, frequently as large as the child, filled with sweets, pens, crayons, and so on.

Fasching

The word *Fasching* is assumed to be a derivation of the Middle High German *vaschanc* or *vastschang* (*Fastschank*), the last drink served before the Lenten fast. Historically, during Fasching, or carnival, the lower classes were allowed to wear costumes and masks and to mimic and mock the aristocracy and heads of Church and state without fear of retribution. Then things got out of hand, the custom was forbidden, and the Empress Maria Theresa decreed at one point that masks would no longer be allowed in the streets; whereupon the revelry was moved indoors. This was the beginning of the splendid balls for which Vienna has become so famous.

More than three hundred balls are staged during the Viennese Fasching. The season begins with the Emperor's Ball in the Hofburg, the former Imperial Palace, where costumed waiters greet the guests and a sumptuous dinner is served in beautifully decorated surroundings. The guests, in traditional Fasching spirit, waltz into the night.

Also hosted at the Vienna Hofburg are the physicians' Ärzteball, the ball of the Vienna

Kaffeesieder (coffee brewers), and the Rudolfina-Redoute. Gloriously decorated with flowers, the Rathaus (town hall) hosts the Blumenball (flower ball). The Vienna Philharmonic holds the Philharmonikerball in the Musikvereinsaal, whose building also hosts the world-famous New Year's Day Concert. The high point of the season, however, is the Opernball at the Vienna Opera House, where guests from around the world are entertained with dining and waltzing far into the night. The Opernball is broadcast across the world, and it is the dream of many a young person to appear at this very formal and traditional event. Preparation for a ball is a serious matter, and almost all young Austrians complete a course in ballroom dancing. Dresses are white, and sparkling crystal tiaras adorn the heads of young ladies as they enter the converted Opera House with their partners for the traditional opening Polonaise. General dancing may not take place until the official dance master announces "*Alles Walzer!*"

FAMILY OCCASIONS
Birthdays
In Austria it is customary on your birthday to take some refreshments into the office to celebrate with your colleagues. If you are invited to

someone's home to celebrate their birthday, a handshake and congratulations are enough. Special birthdays, such as the fortieth or sixtieth, are celebrated in style, usually at the local *Gasthaus* or restaurant. Austrians also celebrate their *Namenstag* (saint's name day), and again congratulations are enough.

Weddings

Weddings in Austria come in many different styles. The most traditional take place in the countryside, where the lucky couple may be captured and held to ransom, and awoken by shots from a cannon or a brass band. Austrians frequently have two weddings: a civil marriage and the religious ceremony. They wear the wedding ring on the third finger of the right hand, and the engagement ring on the third finger of the left hand.

Funerals

Funerals are serious and solemn occasions in Austria. The funeral procession is often accompanied by local dignitaries and a brass band. It is usual to wear black, and large wreaths are the norm, rather than floral tributes. The majority of funerals are burials—cremation is not as common as in Britain and the U.S.A.

chapter four

MAKING
FRIENDS

Friendship in Austria, as in Germany, is
something very special, and "*Freund*" is a term
that is used with care. Most Austrians have a
small, closely knit circle of friends and a wide
network of acquaintances. Frequently friends
are those from school or university days.
Americans and Britons appear to have many
more friends, but the relationship is
much looser. The German
philosopher and writer Friedrich
Schiller said that it is only
possible to have as many
friends as fingers on your right
hand. Therefore it is important that
you, as a visitor, realize that it will
take time to make an Austrian
friend, but once you have made one you will
have a friend forever.

American and British people have always
found it easy to discuss their working lives
openly in a social situation. In Austria, as we
have seen, there is a clear separation between

social and working life, and it is not considered appropriate either to discuss one's private life at work or to bring work home. Changes in the world of work and the increasing need to work are affecting attitudes, but it is still possible to work for years alongside someone without knowing anything about his or her personal life. Partly this has to do with the language and its formality. Colleagues are addressed as "*Sie*," and Austrians often shocked at the immediate informality of English speakers, though the younger generation are more relaxed. The "*du*" form of address is rarely used in business and colleagues are frequently referred to by their title, such as "Frau Doktor," or "Herr Professor." However strange this may seem to visitors, it is perfectly natural to the Austrians.

Austrians work relatively hard, starting early in the morning, but they do finish on time and enjoy their leisure hours to the full, so the best way to meet people is by finding common interests. Outdoor activities form an essential part of social life. Austrians, like their German neighbors, enjoy going on excursions in large groups, and you may find it possible to join up with one of these. Trips are made to the countryside, to walk or cycle, and then everyone finishes up socializing at a country inn or *Heuriger* (a wine producer's cellar or garden).

JOINING CLUBS

Austrians like to pursue their interests in clubs, and this is one of the best ways to make friends. Decide on an interest, then find a club that will cater to you. Details of all such clubs will be found at the local town hall. Austrians particularly like to dance and attend fashionable balls, so learning to dance or improve one's dancing technique is an ideal way to meet people. Then the institute of further education, the *Volkshochschule*, or People's High School, offers a variety classes for all comers. Also, in many towns and cities there are clubs for foreigners, either at the local university, or associated with Rotary or Lion and Lioness organizations. Even if it is not your intention to seek out people of your own nationality, it is worth seeing what these clubs have to offer, because the more people you meet, the wider the potential circle becomes.

GREETINGS

Handshakes are a matter of course in Austria, both on arrival and on departure, as is the use of surnames and titles. Titles, as we have seen, are very important, and one must be sure to be correct and aware of the titles people have. For example, you may meet a Herr Professor Doktor Freundlich, and you should address him as such, and his wife as "Frau Professor," whether or not she has a title of her own. American and British business or academic people denote their titles by initials after their names; in Austria it is advisable to have a business card that clearly states both your job title and your academic or professional qualifications and/or title. This can be used on social as well as business occasions, and saves time. Austrians are still impressed by the number of titles an individual has—a tendency that stems from the days of Empire. The word "general" has different significance in German from English; thus the General Secretary of a company in Great Britain may be a relatively ordinary employee with a broad job specification, whereas in Austria he or she is a very important individual.

Austrians, like Germans, have maintained this formal mode of address for much longer than their American and British counterparts.

Du and Sie

Many languages make a distinction not just between the singular and plural pronouns "you" but between the formal and informal "you." In German the informal "you" is *du*, and is used only for family, close friends, and small children. *Sie* is used for everyone else. English speakers frequently slip into the *du* form, and this may be viewed as a gaffe. As acquaintances get to know each other better they may switch to using *du*, but only if the older person invites the younger to use this form. This may be formally acknowledged by linking arms and clinking glasses of wine or beer.

In some remote country areas you may notice that you are being addressed in the *du* form, but this is an example of local idiom, rather than a sign of intimacy.

Greetings on the Street and in Shops
In country areas it is normal to greet anyone one you meet or pass in the street with "*Grüss Gott*" ("God greet you"). On entering a store or restaurant it is usual to greet everyone with "*Grüss Gott*," "*Guten Morgen*," or "*Guten Tag*," and "*Auf Wiedersehen*" or "*Auf Wiederschauen*" on leaving. If you pass guests in a restaurant eating a meal it is customary to greet them with "*Mahlzeit*," which comes from "*Gesegntes Mahlzeit*," meaning "a blessing on this meal." Some people say, "*Guten Appetit*."

ATTITUDES TO VISITORS
On the whole, Austrians are friendly and hospitable to foreigners, but there is a darker side to their nature. There is some distrust of

strangers, especially in rural areas and away from the more cosmopolitan eastern parts of Austria. Historically, of course, there have always been visitors here from all parts of Europe and beyond.

Austrians particularly welcome visitors who speak German, and are very patient and complimentary even if only a few words are spoken. They view with some suspicion those visitors or immigrants who refuse to converse in German or show any willingness to integrate. Like other prosperous European countries, Austria has become home to many less fortunate people and has been a generous host to European refugees for decades.

INVITATIONS

Generally, Austrians prefer to meet friends in a restaurant, *Gasthaus*, or *Heuriger* rather than to invite them home. It is not usually expensive to eat and drink in these establishments, and there is always a relaxed atmosphere. Austrians, both men and women, are happy to pay their way, so it needs to be made quite clear from the outset if you are inviting them as guests and intending to pay for them.

Invitations home are reserved for special occasions, and although these will also be relaxed events the hosts will work very hard to impress their guests with both their home and the food. Austrians are famous for their hospitality at home. The best china and silver will be used, and everything will be formally arranged. You will probably not get a tour of the house.

An invitation to someone's home is an honor, and you should be punctual. Being a few minutes late is acceptable: *die akademische fünfzehn Minuten* ("the academic fifteen minutes") is a well-known phrase originally relating to university lectures, which are supposed to last for one hour, but actually are only forty-five minutes long.

You should always offer to remove your shoes on entering someone's house. Outdoor shoes are often not allowed indoors, in which case you will be expected to take yours off. You may be given some slippers.

ENTERTAINING

There are various forms of entertaining in Austria. You may be invited to "*Kaffee*," either at 10:00 a.m, or, more usually, at 3:00 or 4:00 p.m. This is supposed to last a few hours. Coffee and tea will be served, and later you may be offered something alcoholic.

In the country the guest may be invited to "*Jause*" (pronounced "yowsa.") This is a "snack" in the early evening. Do not be taken in by this word. There will be enormous amounts  of cold meats and sausage, salads, pickles, and bread, followed by a dessert. You will be expected to stay for some hours, and in the week it is fine to leave by 10:00 p.m., but on weekends you should expect to be there much longer. Toasts are frequently drunk during the evening, the toast being "*Prost!*" or "*Zum wohl!*" (pronounced "prorst" and "tsoom vorl").

After the meal an important part of the evening is just sitting around the table and chatting.

GIFT GIVING

The giving of gifts in Austria is reserved for special occasions, and business gifts are somewhat frowned upon. If you are invited to someone's home, it is appropriate to bring a small gift for your hosts. Bring wine only if it is special and unusual. Chocolates are always acceptable, as are flowers. There is, however, a definite etiquette concerning flowers. The number and color can be significant. It is always best to ask the florist to prepare a bunch and state exactly the purpose of the flowers. This will avoid any embarrassment later.

MANNERS

Good manners and polite behavior are extremely important, and there are codes that must be adhered to, especially in Vienna. Men stand up as a mark of respect whenever another guest arrives, but the old-fashioned "*Küss die Hand, gnädige Frau*" ("I kiss your hand, gracious lady"), when a gentleman would bow deeply over a lady's outstretched hand, is fast disappearing. Men precede a woman when entering a restaurant, help her with her coat, hold the door open for her, and walk on her left-hand side when out of doors, or between her and the road. The "*Bussi-Bussi*" (kiss on the cheek) has become popular in some circles, but is somewhat frowned upon as not being genuine.

Generations of young Austrians have attended a *Tanzschule* (dance school) to learn not only ballroom dancing but also how to behave. Balls are still an important part of the winter social calendar, and people love to dress up and attend these gatherings. Such is the prestige of some of these dance schools that their names have entered into local vocabulary. The Elmayer Tanzschule is synonymous with the standard of polite behavior expected by today's society. This might appear somewhat old-fashioned, but such is the reputation of this establishment that many large international organizations have invited Thomas Elmayer, grandson of the original owner, to hold seminars on correct conduct and etiquette for senior managers. Elmayer's tradition is annually on show in the famous annual Opernball, which is televised throughout Europe and Japan.

chapter five

THE AUSTRIANS AT HOME

In Austria there is a sharp contrast between the formality of work and the relaxed mode at home. The Austrian is generous, friendly, accommodating, and, above all, *gemütlich* (of which, more below).

HEIMAT

Austrians are very committed to their own particular region and homeland—their *Heimat*. They are proud of their region, which they consider to be superior to all others, and when they are introduced they will immediately say where they come from. All regions have their own characteristics, and the inhabitants reflect this. There is a general but good-humored animosity toward Vienna, as it is the seat of national government, but for their part the Viennese consider all the regions to be provincial and narrow-minded. Competition is healthy and regionality has become a good source of

storytelling and jokes. This is where their parents
and forebears lived, and where they were brought
up and educated, and throughout their lives they
keep the connection going. However, Austrians
have a different attitude to their *Heimat* from that
of the Germans. As the renowned Austrian
essayist Hans Weigel once wrote, "Whereas other
nations love their homeland an Austrian is
married to his; and as in a marriage really begins
to appreciate it when he is separated from it."
Those who care most for Austria are those living
abroad. This is partly due to nostalgia for the
imperial past, before Austria's borders were
changed by international wars and disputes.

GEMÜTLICHKEIT

This is a difficult term to explain. An abstract
noun, it is usually translated as "coziness," but it
actually conveys much more than this. It carries
the notion of belonging, social acceptance,
cheerfulness, the
absence of anything
hectic, and time spent
in a place of this
description, which
might be an entire
home or a *Heuriger*, a
garden, or just a living

room. People with similar attributes can also be described as being *gemütlich*.

HOUSING

Home ownership is increasing in Austria, with just over 56 percent of all Austrians owning their own houses or apartments, either as private individuals or under the auspices of ownership cooperatives.

The percentage of home ownership is higher in rural areas than in urban areas and higher in western and central Austria than in the east. In urban areas, apartment houses are much more common than single-family dwellings. Renting is more common in cities and in eastern Austria. Lessees have considerable legal rights to protect them and provide for the regulation of rents. The building and ownership of apartment buildings by the municipality is common in cities such as Vienna, which traditionally have Social Democratic local councils. Older houses are traditionally extremely large—in fact one sometimes feels lost in the space. They are, of course, costly to heat, especially in the Austrian winter. Many have either been converted into apartments or are only partially inhabited. Modern Austrian apartments may be slightly smaller than their equivalents elsewhere, but their ceilings are all much higher. There is usually a generously sized kitchen with a dining corner for the family. A small sitting room is usually reserved for guests and celebrations. Most apartments and houses have a cellar for storage.

By 2000 almost 15 percent of Austrians had a "second residence," used predominantly for recreational purposes. This term, however, describes anything ranging from garden plots with huts (*Schrebergarten*), located on the outskirts of the cities, to old properties in rural communities and newly built one-family houses in the country.

SOCIAL RESPONSIBILITIES

Life in Austria is more relaxed than in Germany and not as ordered, but there are still rules and regulations. For example, in a town or city you should cross the road only at a pedestrian crossing and when the pedestrian light is green. On public transportation everyone is expected to have a valid ticket, and is trusted and expected to conform.

Many of the rules and regulations do seem to make life easier and more productive. Austrians have many communal responsibilities that involve household duties. Communal hallways must always be left clear. There is a shared responsibility for the cleaning of communal staircases and halls, and the sweeping of footpaths is a legal requirement. Consideration for one's neighbors is essential, and one should always warn them in advance—or invite them—if one is having a party.

The disposing of household garbage can be arduous. The local council charges for the collection of all waste materials, which must be sorted according to category; thus glass, plastic, paper, aluminum, tin, organic waste, and general garbage should each be placed in a separate container or, in the countryside, delivered to a central waste disposal site on a weekly basis. The purchase of certain products in glass or plastic bottles requires a deposit that can be reclaimed when the clean empty container is returned to the supermarket. The system of recycling is complicated, and visitors can find it difficult at first. Do not put household waste in a communal waste bin. Some visitors have been publicly scolded for doing this. It's an effort, but Austrians accept that this is how things should be.

Sorted!

Recently an English family spent a month's vacation in Austria. The disposal of garbage became a major issue. Empty beer bottles had to be returned to the local supermarket; wine bottles had to be disposed of in a bottle bank; newspapers had to be put into a special bin; plastic had to be separated from other waste—and this was extremely difficult as some packaging was deemed to be plastic and some not—aluminum foil had to be stored; and garden waste was otherwise to be disposed of. They soon got used to it, however, and by the end of their stay it had become second nature to sort their waste.

Ecological awareness is high on the agenda, and extends into many walks of life. Supermarkets don't supply free bags to carry shopping, so bring your own, or buy them. There are some personal restrictions that can impinge on an individual's freedom, such as when you can mow the lawn, wash the car, or play a radio out of doors.

RENTING AN APARTMENT

If you are staying in Austria for a while, you may wish to rent an apartment. These can be found in newspaper advertisements under the "*Immobilien*" section. Most advertisements will state the monthly rental, the size of the apartment, whether it is furnished or partly furnished, and will usually indicate if there are additional charges (*Betriebskosten*) for water, heating, maintenance, and so on, or if all of these are included in the monthly rental. If the advertisement does not mention these, you should assume that they are not included. Electricity and gas are usually separate extra charges. Central heating is frequently centrally controlled in apartment blocks, with the possibility of adjustment in one's own apartment, and most homes have effective window insulation.

One way to avoid part of the hassle of apartment hunting is to use an agency. The agent will probably speak English, and will have done the preliminary legwork. The properties the agencies show often have a lower monthly rental than those rented directly through landlords. The downside is that an agency will charge a commission, which may be the equivalent of up to three months' rent.

Once you have seen an apartment you want, and stated your interest, there may be a few days' delay while the landlord continues with his scheduled appointments and decides whom he wants as a tenant. He will then call the chosen person and set up a time to review and sign the contract. Unless you speak good German, you should take along a German speaker who is familiar with the standard clauses, so that they can translate the contract, which can be quite lengthy. A security deposit (two or three months' rent) is usually required with the signing of the contract—either in cash, or by bank transfer.

Moving In
Austria works on the metric system. Be aware of the measurements of your furniture and of your new apartment, because your favorite armchair brought from home may not go through the door into your new living room. On the plus side, Austrian beds are larger than British or American beds, and are extremely comfortable. Be warned that bed linen brought from America or Britain may be too small for an Austrian bed.

Many Austrians just use an ordinary saucepan to heat water, and you may not find a kettle provided in your apartment.

Austrian plugs are two-pronged and use 230 volts and 50 herz. The PAL B system is used for televisions. Americans will need to bring adaptors or buy their TV or video locally. The British will only need to bring plug adaptors. American DVDs are not compatible with European machines. Computers should have an adaptor, but check before you leave home.

DAILY LIFE AND ROUTINES

The Austrians get up earlier than most other Europeans, generally around 6:00 to 6:30 a.m., and may be at work by 7:00 or 8:00 a.m. Public transportation runs regularly from 5:00 a.m. The Austrian breakfast is an important meal, and will consist of bread or rolls with slices of ham, sausage, or cheese, or yogurt, accompanied by tea (traditional or herbal), coffee, and milk.

School commences at 7:00 or 8:00 a.m. Children usually take a small packed lunch and return home early in the afternoon. After-school care is now becoming more widely available.

In Austria lunch is traditionally the main meal of the day, and may consist of soup, followed by hot meat, fish, or vegetables, and salad. There is a growing interest in vegetarian food.

In the afternoon people often have a *Jause*, or snack, consisting of coffee and cakes. The Austrians are renowned for their gateaux (*Torte*), which are usually extremely rich and are served with whipped cream (*Schlagobers*).

Supper is often a light meal of cold meats and cheese with pickled vegetables, served with bread. Beer, wine, cider, or tea is usually drunk at this time. Supper is early, usually around 6:00 p.m., but if you have been invited for a drink, expect to be served small delicacies throughout the evening. Austrians generally go to bed early during the week, by 10:30 p.m. at the latest. Don't telephone people after about 8:30 p.m. This is not usual practice, and you may upset your friend or acquaintance.

Bounds and Boundaries

In Austria, one's home is one's castle. There are clear boundary divisions. If you are visiting a house with a front garden, entry is usually obtained by pressing an electronic bell at the garden gate. Many Austrians, we have seen, don't like outdoor shoes worn in their homes, so remember to offer to remove your shoes as soon as you go in.

Guests will be ushered into an informal and friendly room, but the rest of the house will not be open to visitors. Generally each home has an entrance hall, and the doors leading off this are normally kept closed. Children often come to greet a guest and then disappear to their own rooms.

The traditional Austrian housewife is generous and welcoming, and will often have baked delicious fresh cakes specially for the visitor. However, an increasing number of women now work, and the pressures of modern life mean that many make full use of the local *Konditorei*, and buy excellent ready-made cakes.

FAMILY LIFE

By the early 1970s there was a marked change in the size and shape of the traditional Austrian family, and in attitudes toward the ideals of marriage. A sharp drop in the birthrate and a decrease in family size were accompanied by a greater prevalence of single people, single-parent families, cohabitating couples, marriage without children, and divorce. This trend has continued, and grown. One reason for the rise in the unmarried population is the increasing number of educated women who have professional and economic alternatives to traditional wife-and-mother roles. Another reason is that as cohabitation without marriage has become more frequent it has become more socially acceptable. Those who marry often do so at a later age than previous generations.

The declining number of marriages is accompanied by a rising divorce rate. The divorce rate was highest in Vienna and lowest in Tyrol, an indication that traditional and religious values are weaker in urban areas, and are more persistent in traditional Alpine regions. Women who are employed outside the home and have their own sources of income show a greater readiness to divorce than "traditional" wives.

Illegitimacy has also become more common. These social changes are viewed by some with great apprehension. For them the increasing rate of illegitimacy, cohabitation, single-parenting, divorce, and the decreasing birth rate represent a crisis for the traditional religious and social values on which the family is based. For others the diversification of lifestyles is an inevitable consequence of the modernization of Austrian society, as well as part of the more general development of a more pluralistic society, in which no particular lifestyle enjoys a position of predominance.

Large families are most common among farmers, who have a historical and economic tradition of having many children, and among working-class women with little education.

EDUCATION

Education in Austria is free. Private schools exist, but are in the minority. The Austrian education system seeks to furnish the student with a

broader and deeper knowledge base than that
available in the U.S.A. or Britain. The aim is to
create a skilled and educated workforce, but
recently Austria, like other European countries,
has suffered from high youth unemployment.
The relationship between teacher and student in
Austria is far more formal than in Britain, for
example. There is greater emphasis on academic
study and less pastoral work.

Education in Austria is considered very
important, and parents take a great interest in
their children's progress. The origins of the state
education system go back to the school
education system go back to the school
reforms introduced by Empress Maria
Theresa in 1774, which provided the
foundation of education for all,
with six years of compulsory
schooling. In 1869 compulsory
education was extended to eight years.
This was further extended in 1962,
when it was raised to nine years.

After four years of primary school (*Volksschule*),
ten-year-olds move on to either a comprehensive
secondary school (*Hauptschule*) or a higher
secondary school (*Gymnasium*).

After four years at a *Hauptschule*, a one-year
polytechnic course may be pursued. Subsequently,
a start may be made on tuition at a vocational
school, accompanied in parallel by on-the-job

training. Alternatively, after finishing *Hauptschule*, pupils may change to the four-year senior course at a general higher secondary school or conclude their training at a vocational secondary school, taking at an intermediate level a two-to-four year course, or a five-year course at a higher level.

The *Gymnasium* offers an eight-year course. After completing four years at the junior level the pupil may change to an intermediate level or higher level vocational school. Both types of school conclude with the *Matura*, a form of diploma that entitles one to admission to a university. There are special admission requirements for art colleges and for the Academy of Visual Arts.

The task of the vocational schools is to provide specialized training for vocations in specific areas as well as a general education. A complete vocational course takes two to five years. The choice of vocational schools ranges from commercial colleges and business schools to colleges offering vocational training in social work, as well as agricultural and forestry colleges, and an extremely diverse group of colleges and schools providing training for technical, commercial, and artistic professions. Successful conclusion of a course at one of these institutions is recognized as a qualification to pursue the vocation in question. It is also possible to switch from one branch to another within the school system.

As a result of the introduction of greater autonomy in schools with regard to the subjects taught, streaming can be initiated to cater to the differing abilities of the pupils in German, mathematics, and foreign languages. With the freedom to draw up their own timetables, schools can create their own profiles by emphasizing certain subjects, such as the arts or sports.

College students often study part-time while working to support themselves through their studies, and it is not unusual for someone to reach their late twenties before finishing their degree or gaining another qualification.

CONSCRIPTION

National service is compulsory for Austrian males, and is not popular. Much ingenuity goes into avoiding or postponing it. Men are obliged to serve six months, followed by a total of sixty days of refresher training in the reserves. Each reservist receives training over a twelve-day period every second year during his first ten years of reserve duty, generally not extending beyond the time he reaches his mid-thirties. Conscripts can choose to serve seven months instead of six, and have a shorter reserve obligation. Some may serve their full obligation of eight months at one time and have no reserve obligations, but this is at the army's discretion.

Under a 1974 law, conscientious objectors can be assigned work as farm laborers, medical orderlies, or other occupations in lieu of military service. Exemptions from service are liberally granted. Conscripts usually attain the rank of private first class by the completion of initial training. Those with leadership potential may serve a longer period to obtain noncommissioned officer (NCO) status in the militia. Those volunteering for the career service can, after three to four years, apply to attend the NCO academy and later a senior NCO course to qualify as warrant officers.

The military personnel system is an integral part of a comprehensive civil service system. The nine officer ranks, from officer candidate through general, correspond to grades I through IX of the civil service system. The highest grade, IX, may be occupied by a section chief (undersecretary), a career ambassador, or a three-star general. A grade VIII position may be held by a departmental counselor, a career minister, or a brigadier general. Salary levels are the same for civil and military personnel in the equivalent grades, although various allowances may be added, such as flight pay or hazardous-duty pay.

Promotion is not based solely on merit but on level of education, and seniority.

Today conscripts play a major role in the patrolling of national borders, mainly to deter illegal entry into Austria. In national emergencies such as floods the army actively supports local agencies such as the fire department.

Women have never been accepted for service in the Austrian armed forces.

COMPLAINING

Be prepared for the Austrians to grumble about the cost of living, high rents, and bad behavior, and to voice their opinion about most subjects. It is said that Austrians complain a lot, but do not do anything to change matters—it is very unusual for anyone to make a formal complaint.

CHANGING LIFESTYLES

Many changes are taking place in Austria today. The collapse of Communism in her near neighbors has brought a huge influx of migrant workers and shoppers; at times the local inhabitants have difficulties absorbing these new people and tensions have arisen. During recent election campaigns, political parties on the far right have sought to make "immigration and assimilation" a major issue. The Viennese, however, are somewhat more relaxed about this and are reminded of the days of the Habsburg Empire, when it was usual and easy to commute from Bratislava or Sopron. These conditions have re-created the multicultural city Vienna once was. Elsewhere in Austria, especially in rural areas, difficulties sometimes occur.

As we have seen, Austria has experienced a significant rise in single-parent families and also a huge surge in the number of retired people. In 2006 Austria had 1.7 million retired and a workforce of 2.77 million. This clearly is provoking much discussion about the age of retirement and the care provision for retired people. As in the rest of Western Europe, there has been a significant rise in the number of people living together without getting married and also the number of individuals living alone.

TIME OUT

Austrians benefit from having a generous amount
of free time. They work hard and play hard,
starting and finishing work early. For many the
weekend starts at noon on Friday, and the rush
hour gets under way as people head for the
countryside. There are a large number of public
holidays and Austrians have developed the habit of
creating long weekends that stretch a public
holiday into four days, if possible. If a holiday falls
on a Thursday or Tuesday people do not work on
the Friday or Monday. (Unfortunately there is no
replacement for holidays that fall on the weekend.)

Annual leave entitlements are generous, and
most Austrians travel abroad at least once a year,
often to long-haul destinations, and take
short breaks away as well, both at home
and abroad. In spite of being very
health conscious, they are great sun
lovers. Walking, hiking, or cycling in
the summer and skiing in the winter
are all very popular. The numbers of
vacationers are increased by retired people, of

whom there are some 1.77 million, many of
whom are still relatively young.

SHOPPING

Austrians enjoy shopping, and depend much
more on local specialty stores than people in the
U.S.A. or Britain. Austria is unique in that most
people try to buy only Austrian food products. All
meat, dairy, and vegetable products meet an
exceptionally high standard, and even
supermarkets offer locally produced goods.
"Product of Austria" is clearly stamped on all
produce. Genetically modified crops are
not available in Austria. Only exotic
fruits and foods are imported.

Austrians value the quality of fresh food,
and appreciate seasonal variety. The onset
of the asparagus and mushroom seasons are
greeted with overwhelming enthusiasm. In most
towns and villages there is a market selling
vegetables, fruit, meat, fish, oil, and *schnapps*.
Organically grown produce is in great demand
and of a very high quality.

Take your own basket or bags, as shops and
supermarkets do not provide these. You can buy
plastic bags in a supermarket, but packaging is
kept to a minimum because of recycling
regulations. Austrians greet everyone in the shop

with a "*Grüss Gott*" or a "*Guten Morgen.*" "*Auf Wiedersehen*" is the friendly parting phrase.

Saturday and Sunday Closing

During the week shops open at around 8:00 or 9:00 a.m. and close at 6:00 p.m. However, many shops, particularly in the countryside, open earlier—bakers, for example, open at 6:00 a.m.— but close between 12:00 noon and 2:30 p.m. for lunch. On Saturdays shops can stay open until 6.00 p.m. but many close at lunchtime. On Sundays, not only shops but also supermarkets and newsdealers in or near larger towns and cities are closed. Bakers open for a few hours in the early morning. Newspapers can be bought from "help yourself" pouches that are tied to lampposts in most urban streets. Otherwise, the only shops open on Sunday are twenty-four-hour gas stations, frequently only those with automatic payment machines.

BANKS

Banking hours on weekdays are from 8:00 a.m. to 12:30 p.m. and 1:30 p.m. to 3:00 p.m., and are extended on Thursdays to 5:30 p.m. Banks do not open on Saturdays or Sundays.

Cash can be withdrawn around the clock at some 3,000 cash dispensers all over the country.

In some country areas the machines are inside the bank, but can be accessed even when the bank is closed. National and foreign Maestro cards (cash cards) are accepted. Other automated teller cards are national and foreign MasterCard, American Express, Visa, and Diners, as well as the Cirrus and Visa-Plus cash cards that belong to this payment system. There is no "cash back" system.

The currency is the euro, which replaced the Austrian schilling in 2003. Most of Austria, especially in the countryside, is a cash-driven society, and most transactions are paid for in cash. Credit cards are accepted in cities and tourist centers by numerous hotels, restaurants, shops, and gas stations. The credit cards accepted are indicated by the logos displayed on the door or exterior facade of the business.

Most Austrians have a *Girokonto* (checking, or current account) and a *Sparkonto* (savings account). Bills are paid from the *Girokonto* or are paid directly into accounts using just the giro number. People do not use personal checks, and most would use a debit rather than a credit card.

FOOD AND DRINK
Eating Out
Austrians love good food, and have a gourmet tradition. The food is generally excellent, and

portions are enormous. Eating and drinking is a major pastime, and people will travel far to visit a reputable restaurant, or to sample a local specialty or seasonal dish. Several restaurants specialize in fish (all freshwater fish, of course), or venison and other game.

There are many guidebooks and magazines devoted to good food and drink. Bear in mind

that restaurants that have achieved a good reputation are frequently crowded, especially on weekends and public holidays, and you may need to book your table in advance.

Remember also that Austrians eat their main meal at lunchtime, early. If a restaurant is still half empty at 12:30 p.m. it is not a good sign. Also, the choice in the evening may be limited. Unless there is a sign stating "*ganztägig warme Küche*" ("hot food all day"), the restaurant may not offer a hot meal after 2:00 p.m. Likewise in country areas it is often not possible to eat after 9:00 p.m. Most restaurants have a *Ruhetag* (rest day), usually on Monday or Tuesday, but in cities this is sometimes Saturday. Also, if you want to go to a small, family-run restaurant in vacation time, make sure that it is open. It is not unusual for a local shop, restaurant, or *Gasthaus* to close down for two weeks while the owners and staff go away.

A few guidelines may be needed. You should know that the word *Menu* means the fixed-price set meals (there is usually a selection of two or three at different prices, varying in a number of courses). What the Americans and the British call the "menu" is known in Austria as the *Speisekarte,* or *Karte* for short. This usually comes in two parts—a list of dishes, sometimes covering several pages, and the *Tageskarte,* featuring dishes of the day. Most restaurants will have a *Karte* in English as well as German.

Speisekarte and *Tageskarte* are usually displayed outside restaurants, and you can often tell a great deal from these. The fixed-price meals, usually offered at lunchtime, are often excellent value. Portions may not be as large as the same *à la carte* dish, but are still ample. It is unusual to have a bad meal in Austria. The Austrians enjoy a wide range of dishes, including venison, duck, and fish. Pork is the most common meat, but vegetarian dishes are becoming easier to find.

It is customary for the man to enter a restaurant first and hold the door open for his female companion. It is not usual to stand at the bar—you stand just inside the door until the waiter comes to greet you and show you to a table. You rarely find a nonsmoking room in a restaurant or *Gasthaus.*

Ordering in a restaurant comes in two stages. The waiter or waitress will hand out the *Karte* and immediately take your order for drinks. This gives you a while to sit and sip in comfort while you choose what you want to eat. The waiter or waitress will return in a few minutes to take the rest of your order.

Local new wine is very strong, and most Austrians order a bottle of mineral water as well to accompany their meal. Drink is almost always accompanied by food. "*Prost!*" is the word for "Cheers!" and generally glasses are raised and clinked together.

As all food in restaurants is cooked to order, guests at the same table may be served at different times according to their chosen dish. Start eating—you are not expected to wait until everyone else has been served. Before eating people usually say "*Mahlzeit*" or "*Guten Appetit*" to wish each other a pleasant meal. Austrians, like most Europeans, use knife and fork together when eating.

In busy restaurants, especially in the wine taverns, you may find yourself sharing a table with strangers. This can be fun. People are very sociable, and new friends or acquaintances are often made in this fashion. Eating out in Austria need not be expensive, and entire families often meet for Sunday lunch in a local restaurant.

Waiters and Waitresses

To gain the attention of the waiter or waitress it is usual to raise the arm to catch their attention and if necessary call "*Herr Ober!*" or "*Fräulein!*" To ask to pay, say "*Zahlen, bitte.*" It is quite common for a group to ask for separate bills, but remember what you ordered as the waiter or waitress will need to be reminded. The number of bread rolls taken from the basket on the table will be added to the bill.

TIPPING

A service charge of 10 or 12 percent is included in all restaurant bills, so the leaving of anything extra is a matter of personal choice, but it is customary to round the bill up to the nearest euro and ask for the change you want.

It is also usual to round up the bill for a taxi, where the fare is clearly shown on the meter.

If you want fast food, try a *Würstelstand* (sausage stand) where you may join a crowd of city workers having a spicy sausage served with mustard and a roll. There are also many fast-food chains, mostly frequented by tourists and young people.

The Café Culture

The Austrians drink a great deal of coffee, and coffee culture is at its most developed in Vienna, where you will find many grand coffeehouses. Austrians do not order "coffee" but instead ask for their favorite beverage by name. There are coffee menus listing some thirty different ways of serving coffee.

A coffeehouse is the perfect place to relax, read the newspaper, and enjoy the good things in life. Here you can meet friends, chat, and possibly have a game of chess or cards. There are cafés frequented by writers, artists, actors, opera singers, journalists, and politicians. Here Karl Krauss and Trotsky, among others, sat and observed the comings and goings of their fellow human beings.

Desserts and Cakes

The cakes and desserts of Austria are famous. Try *Sachertorte* (a specialty chocolate cake made according to a secret recipe); *Apfel* (apple) and *Topfen* (sweet curd cheese filling) *Strudel*; *Kaiserschmarren* (a doughy pancake with raisins); *Palatschinke* (pancake); and *Salzburger Nockerln* (a meringue-like dish).

COFFEE MENU

Kleiner Brauner
A small cup of espresso with a dash of milk.

Großer Brauner
A double espresso with a dash of milk.

Verlängerter
Espresso "stretched" with hot water.

Mokka
Very strong black drip coffee.

Melange
The Viennese coffee: half Vienna roast coffee and half steamed milk, sometimes with a dollop of whipped cream.

Franziskaner
Coffee with enough milk to resemble the color of a Franciscan monk's robes.

Kapuziner
Coffee with a little less milk than above, to resemble the color of a Capuchin monk's robes.

Nußbraun
"Nut-brown," a little lighter than above.

Nußgold
"Nut-gold," two shades lighter than a Kapuziner.

Cappuccino
Espresso with steamed milk froth.

Einspänner
A tall espresso and milk, with generous whipped cream topping.

Fiaker
Hot coffee with rum or brandy, often with whipped cream on top; sometimes called a *Pharisäer*.

Türkischer
Coffee boiled in the Turkish style, served in copper cups.

Eiskaffee
Iced coffee with vanilla ice cream and whipped cream.

Alcohol

Austria produces excellent wines, but the quality of the best is still largely undiscovered by the world at large. Austrians enjoy drinking in convivial company and most have a healthy and sensible attitude to alcohol. Bottles of mineral water are always ordered with wine and drivers stick to soft drinks. Austrians have no sympathy for overindulgence, and consider this to be socially unacceptable. There are very strict rules concerning driving and alcohol, and the best advice is, "Don't drink and drive." Many road accidents are caused by drunken driving.

Visitors will have an opportunity to make some wonderful discoveries. A popular place to drink in Austria is a *Heuriger* (a wine producer's cellar or garden). A spray of pine branches hanging outside, with a sign bearing the word "*Ausg'steckt,*" indicates that the wine served is exclusively homemade from this local, usually family-owned vineyard. In Vienna especially, a good evening out or social event naturally includes music, and the typical traditional songs that are played and sung at a *Heuriger* are all about wine and the legendary relaxed mind-set of the Viennese.

In Vienna, Lower Austria, and Burgenland, people prefer wine, whereas in Salzburg, Styria, and Upper Austria the preference is for beer. The Austrians like to eat in the open, and every restaurant or *Gasthaus* has a garden or terrace.

The wine-growing areas of Austria are to be found in the eastern and southern regions, stretching from the Danube basin to the borders of Hungary and Croatia. Austrian wine growers are mainly small, independent producers who specialize in producing good-quality wines rather than mass-production. Austria now has the strictest wine laws in the world, and is also one of the largest producers of organic wines.

The most popular white wine is the Grüner Veltliner. Made from a grape variety found only in Austria, it is a refreshing, easy-to-drink light wine with a slight bite to it. There are other varieties of white wine produced, including Riesling and Gewürztraminer. The areas around Lake Neusiedl produce superior red wines, such as Zweigeld and Blaufränkisch, and have also gained an international reputation for dessert wines of an exceptional standard, including Eiswein. This is made by collecting the frozen berries early in the morning on a frosty late October day and allowing the juices to run out, by means of their own weight, into the barrels. Very small quantities of these wines are made, but they are exquisite. Styria also produces good Rieslings and Chardonnays, as well as a rosé specific to that area, called Schilcher.

Beer is also drunk and produced in Austria, both in quantity and of excellent quality. There are many different types, the most common of which is Märzen, which is roughly equivalent to English lager or Bavarian *Helles*. Local and regional breweries frequently produce dark and specialized beers.

In Upper Austria, Lower Austria, Styria, and Carinthia, a type of cider or perry called *Most* is widely produced, while *Sturm*, a semi-fermented grape juice, is drunk after the grape harvest.

At the close of a meal, *Schnapps* (fruit brandy) is drunk, which is made from a variety of fruits, such as apricots, as well as gentian roots, rowanberries, or various herbs. The produce of small private *Schnapps* distilleries, of which there are around 20,000, is known as *Selberbrennter* or *Hausbrand*.

Austria has a range of excellent fruit juices, and many people like to drink mineral water. There is also a very popular Austrian soft drink, Almdudler, which consists of water, sugar, and herb essences. It was made as an alternative to alcohol but is frequently used as a mixer with wine and beer. The beer version is called a "Radler," and is most thirst quenching.

LEISURE
Most Austrian towns have a tourist office and actively advertise and promote places to visit, and things to do and see. There is a huge variety of activities available, both indoor and outdoor.

Festivals and Theme Parks
In addition to the famous international festivals, each village and town has its own annual festival, fire department festival (*Feuerwehrfest*), or shooting festival (*Schützenfest*). Theme parks are something new in Austria, and there are a number of wonderful days out for young and old—for example the huge permanent amusement park in Vienna (Prater), or the Swarovski Crystal World in Wattens, near Innsbruck.

High Culture

Austria is rich in museums, castles, palaces, and monasteries. Music and theater are of national importance in a way that is hard to find elsewhere in Europe, and the opportunity to participate is enjoyed by all, not just a small middle class.

Austrians have a great sense of occasion. Even the tabloid press devotes many front-page column inches to the opening of a new opera production at the Salzburg Festival. The work of Austrian directors and actors abroad is avidly followed. Theater and opera critics are lavish with praise, but also openly condemn a failed production or role. Each season ORF, the national television broadcaster, presents live performances at peak viewing times of all major musical events, especially from Salzburg, Bregenz, and Mörbisch.

The highlight of the broadcasting year is the world-famous New Year's Day Concert from Vienna. Opera and theater stars are as popular as skiers and pop stars. The federal government subsidizes not only the Vienna State Opera House and the National Theater (Burgtheater), but also the Spanish Riding School of Vienna and the Vienna Boys' Choir.

As well as classical opera, orchestral concerts, and ballet, there is a thriving Austrian Jazz and Folk music scene.

The local and regional subsidies for opera and theater mean that prices are usually reasonable and everybody can go. There are always standing only tickets for €5. There is a very wide audience from all sections of society. Dress for the opera and national festivals is mostly formal, meaning evening dress. It is still important to be seen at these events, and tickets are frequently difficult to obtain.

Popular Culture

Increasingly Austrian radio and popular music are becoming more international and losing their national identity. English songs are played on the radio, although there is a strong Austro Pop culture. This is based on a few very strong artists who have quite a large following.

Following Germany, Austria is very tolerant of the public expression of sexuality. Vienna also has an annual gay "Love Parade."

Sports

Austrians are sports enthusiasts, and most are active participants. They follow a wide variety of sports including soccer, shooting, swimming, athletics, riding, and Formula One motor racing, even though their international successes cannot match those of the Alpine skiers. On an individual basis, they actively participate in jogging, Nordic walking (done with special sticks), swimming, hiking, skiing, and cycling.

Skiing is the national obsession, and most young Austrians learn to ski as soon as they can walk. Austrians take this winter sport very seriously, and the nation waits with bated breath during the World Cup Championships and the Olympics. Austrian tourism and the economy are closely linked to the success of the National Alpine Ski team. The sales of several Austrian ski equipment manufacturers are also dependent on their athletes' success. Austria has been at the top of the international competition table for many years, jealously guarding its reputation and nurturing its rising stars.

Country Pursuits

All Austrian towns and cities are surrounded by green spaces, and the countryside is easily accessible. Most people love to go regularly to the countryside and some who live in cities also own a small place in the country. Hiking and walking, especially in groups, are popular activities, as is cycling. Many retired people make the most of discounted rail fares and walk along mountain paths or cycle along the Danube River. In early summer, before the beginning of the school holidays, large parties of elderly ladies and gentlemen on bicycles wobble gently along the river banks clad in the finest cycling regalia. Those who are fitter climb the steep mountain paths in order to admire the views and glimpse the meadows of wild flowers.

TRAVELING

Austria is mountainous, but even the most remote
village can be reached by well-maintained roads and
public transportation. The infrastructure is excellent,

the rail service punctual,
helpful, and comfortable. Public
transportation in Vienna is
superb and cheap—there is no
need for a private car. The
Austrians love to travel. They
are sociable and considerate,
and usually enjoy talking to

their neighbors on a long journey in a train or bus.

DRIVING

Paradoxically, the normally orderly and obedient
Austrian will give visible rein to his anarchical side
once he gets behind the wheel of a car. Picture this:
you have just driven into Austria, you are motoring
along, enjoying the scenery at a moderate speed.
Behind you, at some distance, are a few other local
drivers. You approach a sharp bend and suddenly an

Austrian car shoots out from behind to pass. The first lesson to learn is that Austrian drivers can be reckless. If you have a right-hand drive take extra care—everyone, even the buses, loves to pass a British car.

This quirk apart, private motoring in Austria is a pleasure. The roads are well marked, in excellent condition, and have clear signs. In order to use the highways you have to display a vignette (a toll card). These can be purchased at a *Trafik* (newspaper or tobacconist's stall) or gas station, and are valid for one day, two months, or a year.

Getting Caught

The police are very strict about enforcing traffic laws, and fines, payable on the spot, are heavy. Make sure you receive an official receipt from the officer issuing the fine. Do not argue, as the fine may well increase. If you park illegally your vehicle may be towed away.

By law you must carry your car documents with you, and a red and white warning triangle in the trunk. If you have an accident, take the contact details and registration numbers of the witnesses. If you have a camera, take photographs from all angles before any vehicles are moved. All traffic accidents involving personal injury must be reported immediately to the police. Accidents involving only material damage do not need to be reported unless the identity of the other party cannot be established, but it is wise to call the police in any case.

ROAD SENSE IN AUSTRIA

- You must drive with dipped headlights at all times.

- Visibility vests are now compulsory in Austria if you need to walk at the side of a highway. They must be carried in the car, not in the trunk.

- All must wear a seat belt. Children under the age of twelve must have an appropriate car seat or booster seat.

- If you normally wear glasses you must carry a spare pair in the vehicle at all times.

- You need to carry your driver's license, your insurance certificate (Green Card), and vehicle registration/ownership papers at all times.

- It is strictly forbidden to use cell phones when driving.

- If there are no signs saying otherwise, traffic from the right has the right of way.

- Pay particular attention when approaching a traffic circle—the vehicles on the traffic circle have priority.

- Traffic congestion starts early in large towns and cities. Expect serious traffic build up from 6:30 a.m., and plan accordingly.

- Austria is a tourist transit country. Expect serious delays during school and public holidays. School holidays in Germany are staggered, and this affects traffic in Austria, so make inquiries before you drive.

- Cyclists are common in towns and cities. Beware of the cycle paths in Vienna, which frequently cross pedestrian rights of way.

- Marked pedestrian crossings are now legally enforced stops. When turning at a junction be prepared for the car in front to brake suddenly to allow a pedestrian to cross.

- Streetcars have priority. If you are behind one when it stops, by law you must wait until all passengers alight and have cleared the street. Don't try to pass it.

- Flashing your lights at an oncoming car does not mean, "I am letting you through," but the opposite, "I am coming through!"

- Parking restrictions are clearly marked. At night, parking lights are required in areas without street lamps. In "blue zones" you need to display a cardboard clock showing the time you parked. Free clocks are available at gas stations. There is always a limit on the length of time you can park.

Drinking and Driving

The alcohol restrictions in Austria are very strict, and are applied ruthlessly. Random breath tests are not uncommon. You are only allowed 0.05 percent of alcohol in the blood. This is frequently the equivalent of one beer. The best advice is "Don't drink and drive." If you must drink, leave the car at home.

Car and Driver's License

These are issued in the federal *Bundesländer* (states) by the Bundespolizeidirektion (Federal Policy Headquarters) and in Vienna by the Verkehrsamt (Motor Vehicle department). If you are from the U.S.A. or Canada you can drive up to a year in Austria on your existing license or an international license. U.K. and E.U. residents can drive on their existing license.

If you need to apply for an Austrian driver's license you will need the following documents:

- Completed *Führerscheinantrag* (Driver's License Application Form)
- *Geburtsurkunde* (Birth Certificate)
- *Meldezettel* (Residence Registration Form)
- *Amtlicher Lichtbildausweis* (Official identification with photograph), e.g. passport
- Old driver's license
- Two passport-sized photographs (35 mm x 45 mm)

- Medical report (for the exchange of driver's licenses from countries outside the E.U.)

Jaywalking

Austrians do not jaywalk, even if there is no traffic. U.K. citizens have difficulty with this, unlike Americans. Failure to wait for a green light will result in other pedestrians reprimanding you, or even a fine from a policeman.

Stopping at pedestrian crossings has now become a legal rule, but Austrian drivers are only just getting used to this regulation, so cross with care.

PUBLIC TRANSPORTATION

Public transportation in Austria is a joy. The rail service is excellent and highly efficient. Public buses meet trains and keep to their allotted timetables. Combination tickets for various forms of transport are available, as well as family tickets. The transportation system in urban areas makes owning and driving a private car almost redundant. For example, the system in Vienna includes bus,  streetcar, rail, and metro, and is extensive, fast, efficient, well coordinated, and cheap.

Austria's many airports are clean and efficient, and serve many cities and destinations worldwide. There are no nighttime departures or arrivals. Transportation from the airports to the city centers is quick and regular.

Trains

The public railway system is extensive, with first- and second-class travel available. The Austrian railway is known as Österreichische Bundes Bahn (ÖBB). There are hourly express trains between major cities called ICE, or IC; some of these

services include cities and large towns in neighboring countries. There are first-class compartments for leisure and business customers. Tickets are checked on the train, where tickets and upgrades can be purchased. All departures and destinations are well posted using the twenty-four-hour clock. Diagrammatic versions of the train give precise platform locations for each individually numbered carriage.

It is always worth making a seat reservation, which can be done through a travel agent or by using the ÖBB Web site. There are several discounted fares available on Austrian railways, some of which can only be purchased outside Austria. There are rail passes allowing unlimited travel for a set number of four to fifteen days, and the Eurail pass, which gives unlimited travel to several European countries. These passes are available for both first- and second-class travel.

Service With a Smile

A few years ago I was traveling across Austria by train, and needed to catch a connection just before my final destination. As bad luck would have it, due to some mishap the train was running late. I consulted the conductor, and he assured me that the connection would be made. He telephoned his colleague on the connecting train, and informed me that it would wait for me. It was already dark as we pulled into the station. "Wait just here," said the conductor, "your train is behind us." The train pulled out, to be followed immediately by the connecting train. A carriage door opened in front of me. "*Guten Abend! Willkommen!*" beamed the new conductor. Now, that's service!

Local Bus and Streetcar Services

All Austrian towns and cities have an excellent bus service and many are augmented by streetcars.

Vienna combines *Strassenbahn* (streetcar), *U Bahn* (metro), *Schnellbahn* (fast urban trains), and bus. There are excellent rural bus services connecting villages and hamlets to the train network. Tickets must be purchased before traveling, either from a machine or in Vienna from the local *Trafik*. You

punch your ticket before you board the bus or *U Bahn*; you punch your ticket in the streetcar in cities where these operate. Austrians trust you to buy a ticket and to validate it. However, if an inspector boards and you do not have a ticket, expect to pay a heavy fine. All-night buses exist only in Vienna, but the *U Bahn* begins before 5:00 a.m. and finishes after midnight. In rural areas bus drivers will accept payment on the bus.

Taxis

Taxis cannot be hailed in the street, and must be booked by telephone. Any hotel, restaurant, or *Gasthaus* will be happy to provide this service. Fares are shown on the meter unless a price has been agreed upon beforehand. Fares to and from airports are reasonable.

WHERE TO STAY

Wherever you stay in Austria you can be assured of a warm welcome, with accommodation that is both clean and efficient. There is nearly always a private bathroom with an abundance of hot water. Austria is well-known for its hospitality and quality of service.

Hotels are regularly inspected and graded according to the facilities offered. Accommodation is generally not expensive, except in city centers and at festival time. There are many *Pensionen* that offer bed and breakfast and can be recognized by the "*Zimmer Frei*" sign outside.

The local tourist office, often at or near the station, can help you find accommodation, but don't leave things too late in the day. Remember that Austrians start and finish work earlier than in other countries, and most tourist offices will be closed by 5:00 p.m. Most towns and villages have a *Vehrkehrsbüro*, or tourist office, which is frequently in the *Rathaus* (town hall). These offices will willingly help you find accommodation in a hotel, *Gasthaus*, or *Pension*. Sometimes they charge a small fee for this service.

It is possible to make inquiries from abroad at the Austrian National Tourist Office Web site, www.austria.info,but this is not a booking facility.

There are campsites throughout the country. For information try the Austrian National Tourist Office or www.campsite.at.

Youth hostels are run by Österreichischer Jugendherbergsverband (Austrian Youth Hostel Association), oejhv-zentrale@oejhv.or.at

You must be a member of the International Youth Hostel Association (IYHA) to stay. OEJHV publishes details of all hostels.

Those interested in climbing or walking in the mountains may wish to stay in Alpine refuges. In any case you must contact the Österreicher Alpenverein (the Alpine Club of Austria) before you set off on any tour. There are very strict rules and regulations governing trekking in the mountains.

HEALTH AND SECURITY

Austria is well stocked with doctors and pharmacies. Pharmacies operate on a rotating basis for night and Sunday duties, and when they are closed they display a notice giving the addresses of the nearest open pharmacies. The Austrian medical system is excellent but expensive, and you should arrange private health insurance. If you are an E.U. citizen your European Health Insurance Card will provide emergency coverage.

If you stay in Austria for a long period, you will be considered a resident, and will have to pay contributions to a local social insurance organization (*Sozialversicherungsträger*). These are often called *Gebietskrankenkasse.* If you are working, your employer will normally deduct the contributions from your salary and make the payments on your behalf. Ask your employer for the details of the scheme, or contact the local health insurance organization. If you are studying, you must have your own private insurance coverage.

If you need to visit a doctor you do not usually have to pay in advance. If you are a student or working full-time in Austria, you have to bring your insurance certificate. It is generally possible to leave a deposit if you need urgent medical help.

If you are covered by private travel or health insurance, you pay via bank transfer. If you want your insurance company to reimburse you, remember to keep the receipts. Not all treatments are covered by public or private insurance. Check with the doctor and/or the insurance company.

Hospital

If you are studying or working in Austria, treatment in a hospital is free except for a small contribution called co-payment, depending on your insurance. When traveling in Austria check with your insurance company prior to departure which treatments and emergencies are covered.

Hospitals and physicians generally do not accept credit cards.

As in Germany, pharmacists have considerable expertise and greater freedom to recommend products. Often you may find that you are offered natural or homeopathic remedies.

Violent Crime
Violent crime is far less common in Austria than in the United States and some parts of Britain. Generally walking around town is quite safe in the evenings and there are no "no go" areas; however, you are always advised to take sensible precautions.

SAFETY PRECAUTIONS
- Be aware of pickpockets, especially in crowded areas.
- Do not carry all your credit cards in one purse or wallet.
- Keep your car locked at all times.
- Do not leave bags unattended.
- In hotels put your valuables and money in the safe.
- Make copies of your driver's license and passport and keep them separately from the originals.

Members of the local police force are usually quite visible and will always offer polite assistance. In the past few years there has been an increase in crime which, with some justification, has been attributed to the large influx of immigrants from Eastern Europe. Here, as in most of Western Europe, organized crime appears to have gained a foothold.

If you are the victim of a crime, report it to the police immediately.

IDENTITY AND RESIDENCE PERMITS
All Austrians carry identity cards and use them when registering at the town hall or library, or when entering children for school. You may use your passport for the first three months of your stay, and if you are a national of a country outside the E.U. you will also require a visa. A longer stay requires a residency permit.

There are three types of residence permit: a visa (for short stays or visits); a stay permit (*Aufenthaltserlaubnis*, for working or studying but not settling in Austria); and a residence permit (*Niederlassungsnachweis*, for settling in Austria).

Like visas, applications for all residence permits must be processed before coming to Austria. Start the application paperwork early, and hand in all the documents personally at the Austrian Embassy or Consulate in your home country.

chapter eight

BUSINESS BRIEFING

The conduct of business in Austria is very similar to that in Germany, and involves diplomacy and protocol. How you behave, dress, and proceed is very important. The business world in Austria is undergoing a major revival. Contracts with and expansion into the neighboring countries of Eastern and Central Europe have accelerated, and Vienna International Airport is becoming the hub of Central Europe.

A number of Austrian companies, such as Red Bull, Swarovski, and Plasser, have an international market and reputation. The situation in Central Europe is extremely fluid, however, and Austrians have discovered that agreements can change. A recently signed and accepted tender for the

 redevelopment of Bratislav Airport by Vienna International has been shelved by the new Slovak government.

Discussions continue, however; such is the pressure to modernize that individual governments

cannot afford to be isolated or ignore Austrian business practice.

The Austrian way of conducting business is to focus on deals and data, in a rather formal, reserved, and structured style. There are still many small, family-run businesses, and these are increasingly operated by the sons and daughters of the original owners. Judgment and tact need to be shown here, using charm and diplomacy when dealing with the older generation and cool business objectivity with the young. The personal relationship one might have had with the original owner is not always forthcoming when dealing with the younger generation. The pace is faster, and people tend to be less patient. There is an element of, "Here's my offer; accept it, or there is no deal."

TIMEKEEPING

In Austrian business culture you are expected to be early for appointments and meetings. To be right on time for a meeting may be interpreted as being late. Meetings have agendas, which are to be followed. Being late for appointments or work is not easily excused, and explanations such as, "I couldn't find a parking place" simply suggest that you did not allow enough time for this eventuality. Always plan to arrive a little early.

WORKING CONDITIONS

Office working hours are, officially, 8:00 a.m. until 5:00 p.m., Monday to Friday, and generally conform to the European thirty-seven-hour week. However, as we have seen, Austrians start the day early and many are at their workplace long before 8:00 a.m. Flexible working hours exist in most

companies, and the foreign businessperson would be well advised to avoid making appointments on a Friday afternoon. It is still quite common for work to cease after lunch on Friday and often impossible to reach an Austrian colleague by telephone after noon. Many switchboards close early, but most workers have a direct line with its own message service or voice mail.

Austrian vacation entitlement is identical to that of Germany—a minimum of four weeks, rising higher with promotion. Austrians usually take their vacations in two blocks to enable them to enjoy the winter as well as the summer season. The main vacation period is July and August and it can be difficult to conduct business during these months.

Sickness and maternity benefits are also generous. New mothers are entitled to sixteen weeks' paid leave, and there are good schemes for paternity leave as well. Workers are entitled to six weeks' fully paid sick leave and can claim regular visits to a *Kur* (health spa) on the basis of medical advice. Many Austrians suffer from *Kreislaufstörung* (circulation problems), which are triggered by changes in the weather or air pressure. This complaint is hardly recognized in the U.S.A. or the U.K., but great attention is paid to it in Austria and Germany.

The idea of working overtime can be viewed quite differently, depending on an organization's culture. Among the younger free-marketeers it may be seen as evidence of a hardworking attitude. However, an Austrian colleague might just as well think that one has been inefficient and unproductive during the day, or has made incorrect projections of the level of work. The Austrians do not appreciate the modern British work ethic of working late into the night.

OFFICE ETIQUETTE AND PROTOCOL
Dress

Workplace style differs according to industry, region, and average age. The generally appropriate form of dress is conservative, but is also stylish, serious, and up-to-date. Young businessmen tend not to wear ties, but smart jackets and jeans. This has now become the office uniform. Even TV hosts read the early evening news dressed in this fashion. However, in general, dressing for an occasion is appreciated. Austrian style is greatly influenced by Italian and French couture. The Austrian businessman likes to dress up, especially for the next prestigious ball.

Forms of Address

You should always acknowledge people with a formal greeting before starting a conversation; the most common being "*Grüss Gott.*" This includes anyone you meet and not just your primary contacts. The formal *Sie* must always be used, and when addressing colleagues make sure that you acknowledge their title. The importance of titles cannot be overstated, and this is reflected on a person's business card. Should someone have two PhDs, say, then this must be acknowledged, and he or she should be addressed as, for example, "Dr. Dr. Huber." Titles ensure respect, so make absolutely certain that your cards bear your title.

WOMEN IN MANAGEMENT

The Austrian concept of "equal treatment" differs substantially from the American idea of "equal rights." Austrian legislation not only aims to establish equality in realms where there is discrimination against women, but it also attempts to provide women with additional benefits to compensate them for "unpaid work" in the household, the dual burden of employment and child rearing, or single parenting. In other words, "equal treatment" involves interpreting equality literally in some spheres and attempting to compensate for the gender-specific inequality of burdens in others.

Women have achieved very high executive positions in both business and public life, and there have been notable female politicians and TV hosts. Although women have held cabinet positions in recent Austrian governments and also ministerial portfolios within the European Union, Austria has yet to have a female chancellor (prime minister) or president. A glass ceiling does still exist, but women are certainly making their mark, especially in public service.

Because Austria is a conservative country, foreign female business executives need to establish their status and criteria at the outset. Memos, letters, and business cards should state clearly your company position and qualifications.

As far as dress goes, it is important to remember that the Austrians are very clothes conscious. Women are advised to dress conservatively at least until they begin to know the company, and then they will be able to adapt their clothes style as they wish.

Austrian executives are especially polite and attentive to their female counterparts, and the older men will observe courtesies that have for the most part disappeared in many Western societies: simple things such as opening the door, standing up as a women enters the room, walking on her left side or between her and the road. In exceptional circumstances, a courtly elderly man may bow low and take a woman's hand to kiss it as a greeting, "*Küss die Hand, gnädige Frau*" (I kiss your hand, Madam). This rarely happens nowadays, but it is a good idea to be ready for it in order to avoid possible embarrassment. This is an example of real Viennese charm.

LEADERSHIP AND DECISION MAKING

The Austrian workplace is hierarchical, and relationships between superiors and subordinates are unequal. Traditionally, management tends to

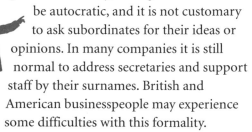

be autocratic, and it is not customary to ask subordinates for their ideas or opinions. In many companies it is still normal to address secretaries and support staff by their surnames. British and American businesspeople may experience some difficulties with this formality.

However, as the younger generation is adopting newer and more democratic management practices, this may change somewhat.

Managers are supposed to lead, and are expected to have more experience than their juniors. Superiors should have a good sense of their subordinates' work. If a superior frequently asks employees for their ideas and opinions, this can be interpreted as incompetence. While staff would certainly appreciate a personable boss, a certain social distance should be maintained between hierarchical levels. Good managers are their employees' mentors, certainly not their friends.

Knowing One's Place

A Viennese boss wanted to thank his staff for completing a special contract on time, and invited them all out for a drink. He arrived an hour late, picked up the bill, paid it, thanked his staff for attending, and promptly left. No one felt insulted.

Decision-making power is usually clearly delineated, either specifically linked to a job's function or through signing over authority. The generation of ideas is often limited to the management cadre or institutionalized through the creation of advisory positions. Initiative is valued, as long as it is within one's own area of responsibility. Employees are expected to ask their superiors for advice or help if a new situation arises that is not outlined in a process document. In return, superiors are expected to have the answers. Some organizations have "comment boxes" to encourage innovation and change.

Relationships with clients or colleagues may be built over time if there are common interests present. Austrians are eager to establish a good working relationship with customers and will disapprove of any member of their team who may harm this by behaving improperly or not meeting the required high standard of conduct.

Nepotism is not encouraged, but is not seen as entirely improper. The appropriateness is evaluated on a case-by-case basis. It is fairly common for employees to put in a request for their employer to take their children or young relatives into the company for internships or short placements for work experience.

Austria's labor market is more flexible than Germany's, and protection against dismissal is not as comprehensive. Austria is a welfare state where employers, trade unions, and government try to resolve problems and issues around the table. Wage negotiations are settled nationally and strikes are unlikely. The privatization of key national industries caused agitation, anger, and protests in the past.

PRESENTATIONS

Austrians appreciate clear, factual, and focused presentations. They like comprehensive background information, references, and testimonials. Be prepared to answer detailed questions, and when answering be as precise as possible. Make sure your paperwork covers every aspect of your presentation. Austrian audiences are not impressed by flashy presentations that give only a broad sweep of the topic. A lack of detailed questions following a presentation could well mean that it was considered neither interesting nor relevant.

SOCIAL PARTNERSHIP

Social partnership is a special feature of Austria, a system of cooperation between representatives of employers' organizations—the Austrian Federal Economic Chamber (WKÖ) and the Congress of Presidents of the Chambers of Agriculture—and the employees' organizations—the Federal Chamber of Workers and Employees and the Austrian Federation of Trade Unions. The chambers are legally constituted interest groups with compulsory membership for employers and employees alike. As a result these bodies are in a very strong negotiating position with the state authorities. Membership in the Federation of

Trade Unions is voluntary. The social partners also jointly determine collective-bargaining agreements, as for example the minimum wage in individual industrial sectors.

Since the Second World War the representatives of employers and employees have worked together to achieve a conflict-free reconciliation of their respective interests. This has resulted in Austria's postwar economic stability, social harmony, low incidence of strikes, and, until recently, low unemployment levels. As elsewhere in Europe, unemployment has risen; in 2006 it was 6.7 percent of the workforce, with the brunt being borne by the young. Successive governments have attempted to address the issue, and recent business expansion into the countries of Central and Eastern Europe has helped to alleviate the situation. Austria is an attractive environment for business expansion.

This combination of democracy, a market economy, and social partnership has fostered a special culture in Austria, and the Austrian political system has been characterized by an atmosphere of compromise and mutual understanding.

PLANNING AUTHORITIES

We have seen that Austria is a federal republic, and that the leader of each region is an elected and paid political official with immense influence and power. In addition, all cities, towns, and districts have an elected and paid *Bürgermeister* (mayor). All decisions regarding planning, commerce, and industry must be agreed with the *Bürgermeister* as well as with the regional authorities. The *Bürgermeister* has a great deal of local power and influence and should always be approached at the initial stage of any business proposition that might involve local infrastructures.

NEGOTIATIONS

Negotiations for a contract will normally be conducted by the executive responsible for that task or section. The chief executive will delegate, and will not generally take part in discussions. The final decision, however, will be left to the Managing Director or Board. A contract will be drawn up, and it is always advisable to have a translation made. The German version should also be examined by a lawyer to ensure that no words or phrases have been misunderstood or misinterpreted.

CONTRACTS AND FULFILLMENT

The Austrian legal system is based on Roman Law, enshrined in statute. Additionally, it relies heavily on German Law in the field of Commercial Law. The General Civil Code, *Das Allgemeine Bürgerliche Gesetzbuch* (ABGB), established in 1811, is one of the world's oldest codes of civil law. Case law does not apply in Austria, but each judge has the freedom to interpret the statutes.

In 2007, a new unified Commercial Law, *Unternehmensgesetzbuch* (UGB), came into force. This abolished national and vested restrictions to conform with European Union requirements. There is now complete freedom as to the form and content of any contract; any remaining restrictions exist principally for the protection of consumers. Contracts may be entered into in writing, by e-mail, or verbally, and are equally binding. The important issue is the willingness expressed by both parties. There are particular requirements regarding contract forms (such as a written form, and certification by a notary) that apply, for example, to credit agreements and insurance policies. Silence should not be taken to imply consent to a contract; in fact silence cannot be interpreted as the acceptance of an order.

It is also important to remember that the transfer of ownership on the purchase or sale of goods occurs not on the signing of the contract but with the delivery of the goods to the purchaser. Austria is also a member of the U.N. convention on contracts, and U.N. contract law applies in cases of international transactions between all member state companies.

THE E-CARD

With the introduction of the E-Commerce Law of 2002, a legal framework has been established for a series of standard functions.

All Austrians receive an E-card. This electronic insurance card replaces the previous paper forms that were required for medical care, and can easily be made to function as the citizen's ID card. The use of the citizen's ID card for legitimization purposes is already supported by many electronic banking systems, eliminating the need to enter a PIN and transaction number (TAN) for transactions.

An Austria-wide register of addresses ensures up-to-date and correct address information at a low cost. The rapid implementation of E-government has earned Austria second place among E.U. member states.

CONCLUSION

Austria has once again become a highly attractive business partner, and is now ranked seventh in the world by OPEC, which is based in Vienna, while Germany ranks twenty-first. Austria's economy is growing faster, and its unemployment rate is significantly lower, than most of its neighbors, although the Austrians themselves still consider their youth unemployment level unacceptably high.

The value generated by an Austrian worker is as much as twice his wages, while a German worker generates 1.4 times his wages, at most. Austrians work longer hours, and corporate tax and nonwage labor costs are low.

As a business location, Austria is now among the best in Europe. Several billion euros are being provided for the expansion of its transportation infrastructure. The country has a beautiful natural environment, and its industrial and economic progress has led to an improvement rather than a deterioration in its quality. Austria is at the forefront of high-tech development and production. It supports the highest share of organic farming in Europe. Research and development of new products to reduce greenhouse emissions and expand the use of renewable energy sources has enabled its industries to secure their international competitiveness and strengthens the country's attractiveness as a business location.

An added attraction is the exemplary social market economy. This social partnership is a relationship based on trust and common understanding and goals. The Austrians are an educated, honest, and hardworking people who can be relied upon to produce goods of exceptional quality and value.

chapter nine

COMMUNICATING

LANGUAGE

The quality of English-language education in Austria is such that almost everyone you meet can speak English quite well; the majority of younger people speak it fluently and without an Austrian accent. Austrians will try to please the visitor by speaking in English. However, they greatly appreciate visitors who make some attempt at German, even the use of phrases such as "*Grüss Gott*," "*Guten Morgen*," and "*Auf Wiedersehen*."

The German spoken in Austria is the same as that spoken in Germany, although there are varying regional dialects and some different words and phrases. The influence of other languages has meant that many foreign words have entered the Austrian German vocabulary. Also, for many years the court language was French. Thus a *Paradeiser* (tomato) in Vienna is a *Tomate* in Germany, an *Erdapfel* (potato) in Austria is a *Kartoffel* in Germany, and an Austrian

Fleischhauer (butcher) is a German *Metzger*. If you intend to stay and work in Austria for some time, it is worth purchasing an Austrian dictionary—an *Österreichisches Wörterbuch*.

The Croissant

Cultural exchange can work both ways. That quintessentially French pastry, the croissant, was originally the Austrian *Kipferl* (crescent), a legacy of the Ottoman presence at the gates of Vienna. It was taken back to France by an appreciative Napoleon.

If you look at older books in German you will notice that many of them are printed in a Gothic typeface, now totally abandoned in favor of standard Roman characters. Handwriting before the Second World War was *Kurrentschrift*, a German script with its own set of characters, which few people nowadays can read. Deciphering handwriting on official documents completed before this period can therefore be a problem, though you may find a class teaching this at the local *Volkshochschule*. This is an  essential skill if you need to read old documents, such as public records and legal papers.

All Austrian children learn standard German, *Hochdeutsch*. This is the educated language of all German-speaking peoples, but among themselves regional dialects prevail. In business circles one would always use *Hochdeutsch*. Most dialects are comprehensible, but there are some difficulties with the very broad dialects of Vorarlberg and Carinthia. There have recently been several attempts to reform and modernize German writing and spelling throughout the German-speaking world, and new regulations have been introduced. However, such is the confusion that it is very difficult to know which version is being used. Austria, at the time of printing, is using the second version of new spellings introduced in September 2004. There have been further revisions but these merely confuse the issue even more. A good German dictionary, such as the Duden, will help.

MAKING CONTACT

The most acceptable way to make contact is with a formal letter of introduction, followed by a telephone call. Don't use e-mail—this tends to get ignored. Cold calling is frowned upon, and regarded as an intrusion.

Job applications should always be typed and sent with a photograph.

COMMUNICATION STYLES

Many Austrians are somewhat reserved toward foreigners on first meeting them, and most find the outgoing and positive attitude of Americans superficial, or even overbearing. The Austrian businessperson is not interested in small talk, or conversations about family and personal matters. The focus is on the business at hand, and may seem overly serious. Young Austrians are far more at ease, flexible, and cosmopolitan in their outlook.

Eye contact is important between people in hierarchical relationships, and it is considered respectful to lower one's gaze now and again. It is customary to shake hands with both men and women when meeting and leaving. Handshakes are firm, and require direct eye contact.

Austrians are direct in their communications, especially in written form, and requests for information are clear and precise. The less direct style of English speakers may appear to Austrians to lack focus, and they may misinterepret this as not requiring a response.

Another factor influencing the Austrian communication style is the unequal relationship between superiors and subordinates—it is not usual to ask subordinates for their ideas or opinions. However, as the younger generation adopts more democratic management practices, the style is starting to change.

Education affects communication style.
Austrians are taught to be clear thinkers,
analytical, and factual, and their communication
is formal, precise, and involved. Meetings are also
more formal than those of their British and
American counterparts.

CONVERSATION

In the right social atmosphere, such as over a
drink or a meal, people are happy to converse on a
range of topics. Discussions are usually
lighthearted, and full of humor and fun.

There are certain topics to avoid unless you
know the company really well. For example, it is
difficult to get people from the older generation
to talk about the Second World War and their role
during this period. Younger Austrians are more
ready to discover what really went on, and are
generally prepared to tackle difficult subjects.

HUMOR

Austrian humor favors wit and irony, although
slapstick also goes over well. The keynote of
Austrian humor is self-deprecation, and a
conviction that things will always turn out
badly—even when they are turning out well. The
Austrians have nurtured the humor of damage

limitation, or graceful resignation, developed by the playwright Nestroy in the eighteenth century. He famously used burlesque, music, wordplay, and the Viennese dialect for incisive social satire. Viennese humor extracts elements of Bohemian surrealism, Hungarian pessimism, the Italian tradition of mimicry and clowning, and the bitter humor of Jewish writers and cabaret artists. This tradition continues today; the cabaret scene in Vienna is extensive and well supported, although even a fluent German-speaker may have difficulty understanding the language and nuances of the broad Viennese dialect.

THE MEDIA

The media landscape is dominated by large companies. In the press sector, the two most popular daily newspapers, *Neue Kronenzeitung* and *Kurier*, together reach more than half of the population. These two newspapers belong to the same holding company, which deals with all aspects of commercial business, advertising, and distribution for both papers.

The Press

Austrians are avid newspaper readers, and follow and discuss the news. There is no censorship. Newspapers do not have any formal affiliation with any particular party, but do have political leanings. More than three million newspapers are distributed every day to a population of some eight million people. More than a million copies are circulated by the *Neue Kronenzeitung* alone; the other two million represent the total distribution of sixteen daily newspapers all over the country, including local and regional papers. The national newspapers are:

Broadsheets
Die Presse (center-right, classical liberal)
Der Standard (center-left, social liberal)
Wiener Zeitung (organ of the Republic of Austria founded in 1703 and probably the world's oldest newspaper)
Intermediate format
Kurier (center, social liberal)
Tabloids
Kronen Zeitung (populist, traditionalist)
Kleine Zeitung (moderate, Catholic-liberal)

There are many other local newspapers and weekly magazines.

TV and Radio
There is only one public broadcaster in Austria, Österreichische Rundfunk (ORF), which enjoys a nationally unchallenged position in television.

Private television operators are limited to the local level, with no market significance whatsoever. In the field of radio, ORF's legal private competitors started operations in April 1998, but have not succeeded in challenging the market leader's position.

There are two ORF television channels and a network of regional stations for both television and radio. Austrians make the most of satellite and cable channels, which enable them to receive most German and Swiss broadcasts. It is also possible to receive CNN, BBC, and Eurosport channels. Most apartment blocks are wired for satellite.

Austria also works on the PAL-B/G system. This is different from the American NTSC and the British PAL systems. You can play PAL videocassettes. It is best to buy a local TV.

Many foreign films and TV programs are broadcast in Austria, but they are mainly dubbed into German.

Austrians pay a license fee for each radio and TV set they use, and need to register these.

The Internet
Austria has a high rate of PC ownership. By March 2005, 56.8 percent of all adult Austrians had access to the Internet at home or in the office. There is a large range of Austrian Internet service providers.

Most hotels make Internet connection freely available. There are also, of course, plenty of Internet cafés.

The ORF and all major newspapers have a well-established Web site, as do all government agencies and regional and local authorities.

SERVICES
Telephones

The telephone system in Austria is very efficient. It is run by Telekom AT, which controls the network. There are also alternative and cheaper systems, such as Skype, or others where you choose a service by dialing the appropriate code before the number you are calling.

Coin-operated phone booths have all but disappeared and are being replaced by phone cards. These you can buy at the local *Trafik* or telephone shop, or from a vending machine at a main railway station or airport. You can make international calls from the post office, using international calling cards or credit cards. Beware of making phone calls from hotels as the surcharges are very high.

When Austrians answer the phone they normally state their name. You, too, should identify your company and yourself. "*Hier spricht Schmidt Ltd.; ich heisse Jones.*" ("This is Schmidt Ltd.; my name is Jones.")

Don't call anyone after 8:30 p.m., unless you know that your respondent keeps later hours than most Austrians.

The country code for Austria is 43, and there are area codes for each part of the country. The codes for the main cities are: Vienna 1; Linz 70 or 732; Graz 316; Salzburg 662; Innsbruck 512; Klagenfurt 463; Bregenz 5574; Eisenstadt 2682. Within the country dial 0 and the area code. From overseas dial 43 and the area code (without the 0). To dial out of Austria you normally dial 00 before the foreign country code.

For directory enquiries, dial 1151. You can also use the Yellow Pages for business numbers, or the phone book for residential numbers.

EMERGENCY TELEPHONE NUMBERS
Fire 122
Police 133
Ambulance/Emergency Doctor 144

Mail

As in Germany, "snail mail" is still very important in Austria. You will notice yellow mailboxes all over the country, and on mountain roads you will see the *Postbus* collecting and delivering mail to remote mountain villages. The postal service is extremely efficient and quick, with next-day delivery the norm, not just in Austria but also abroad. There is only one regular delivery a day, and the postman delivers to mailboxes at garden boundaries or at central points in apartment blocks.

Post offices are open between 8:00 a.m. and 6:00 p.m. Monday to Friday and between 8:00 am and 12:00 noon on Saturdays. However, in some rural areas they may close one day a week. In all major towns the post office remains open longer in the evening and is also available on Sundays.

Post offices offer a wide range of services. They sell all types of stationery, toys, special-issue stamps, and other collectors' items, as well as theater and concert tickets. One can pay utility bills there, and carry out other transactions. The post office will also arrange mail and parcel collection from your home or office.

E-mail is not a widely used form of commercial communication in Austria. There are still many establishments, both public institutions and private companies, where e-mails are simply ignored.

CONCLUSION

How, then, do the Austrians differ from their neighbors—the Germans and the German-speaking Swiss? One could start by saying what they are not. The Austrians are not Germans—their roots and culture embrace more than this single-language identity. And they do not have the determined work ethic or clarity of vision of their larger neighbor. Neither do they possess the fierce independence and democracy of the Swiss. The Austrians have never established a national, as opposed to regional, identity—people think of themselves as being, say, Carinthian or Tyrolean.

The inheritance of the Habsburg reign along the banks of the Danube River has infused the Austrian in a brew that has lasted for centuries, merging and stirring the waters of Germany, Switzerland, the Magyar, Slav, and Italian lands into the complex blend of Austrian identity. "Austrianness" is not a geographical concept but rather the idea of enlightened humanity springing from a wide combination of peoples.

The Austrian nostalgically looks to the past, embraces the rich culture he has inherited, and appreciates the wonderfully beautiful setting of his homeland. The Czech politician František Palacký wrote, "Indeed, if this Austria did not exist, then, in the interests of humanity itself, one would have to hasten to create it."

Austrians are both happy and melancholic. They have developed a highly critical nature, which can express itself humorously in irony and self-deprecation. They may also, at times, show their darker side, and enjoy intrigue and malice. There are no longer recollections of revolutions or freedom fights; there are no great rulers or intellectuals. Austrian collective pride is to be found in the beauty of their scenery, social harmony, relaxed wealth, and cultural heritage. Today's Austrians are a complex people—charming, friendly, engaging, interested in all matters, stimulating to listen to, and challenging in debate—living in a modern, dynamic country with a rich and diverse history and culture.

Appendix: Some Famous Austrians

Empress Maria Theresa, 1717–80
The only female ruler of the Habsburg family, and probably the most successful.

Franz Josef Haydn, 1732–1809
Classical composer and court musician, composer of great symphonic and religious works.

Wolfgang Amadeus Mozart, 1756–91
Composer and court musician, prolific, highly influential, and arguably the most popular composer in the classical repertoire, who wrote symphonies, operas, and chamber and choral music.

Andreas Hofer, 1767–1810
Peasant farmer and freedom fighter for Tyrol. Won battles against the French before being defeated, captured, and executed. He is the symbol of Tyrol.

Franz Schubert, 1797–1828
Classical composer of songs, symphonies, church music, and sonatas, who died at a very young age and became fully appreciated posthumously

Gregor Mendel, 1822–84
Augustinian monk, botanist, and founder of modern genetics.

Anton Bruckner, 1824–96
Classical composer of the late Romantic period, and organist at the monastery of St. Florian.

Johann Strauss, Junior, 1825–99
Composer and "Waltz King."

Bertha von Suttna, 1843–1914
Great advocate of Pacifism, who was awarded the Nobel prize for Peace in 1905.

Sigmund Freud, 1856–1939
Neurologist and founder of the first school of Psychoanalysis.

Gustav Mahler, 1860–1911
Post-Romantic composer and conductor.

Gustav Klimt, 1862–1918
Artist and sculptor who was a prime mover of the Vienna Secessionist movement.

Arnold Schoenberg, 1874–1951
Composer, music theorist, and innovator of the twelve-tone technique.

Ferdinand Porsche, 1875-1951
Automotive engineer.

Hans Moser, 1880–1964
Viennese comic actor, whose films are still very popular today.

Stefan Zweig, 1881–1942
Novelist, short story writer, and biographer, widely translated and still popular today.

Erich von Stroheim, 1885–1957
Filmmaker and actor.

Erwin Schrödinger, 1887–1961
Nobel prizewinning physicist, creator of Schrödinger's Equation.

Ludwig Wittgenstein, 1889–1951
Philosopher who worked for many years at Cambridge and was renowned for his work on Logics and the Philosophy of Mathematics.

Wolfgang Pauli, 1900–58
Nobel prizewinning theoretical physicist, known for the discovery of the Exclusion Principle.

Karl Popper, 1902–44
Influential philosopher of science, author of *The Open Society and its Enemies*.

Konrad Lorenz, 1903–89
Behavioral scientist and founder of ethology. Received the Nobel prize for Medicine and Physiology in 1973.

Kurt Gödel, 1906-78
Logician, mathematician, and philosopher of mathematics.

Billy Wilder, 1906–2002
Screenwriter, film director, and producer.

Hedy Lamarr, 1913-2000
Actress and communications technology innovator.

Friedensreich Hundertwasser, 1928–2000
Artist, sculptor, and architect, famous for his municipal buildings in Vienna, which include housing projects and a massive incinerator and heating furnace.

Ernst Fuchs, 1930–
Painter, sculptor, architect, composer, poet, singer, and co-founder of the Vienna School of Fantastic Realism.

Romy Schneider, 1938–82
Film actress.

Arnold Schwarzenegger, 1947–
Bodybuilder, film actor, and Governor of California.

Nicki Lauda, 1949–
Formula One world champion and entrepreneur who now runs a successful fleet of low-cost aircraft.

Franz Klammer, 1953–
Greatest alpine downhill skier of modern times, world and Olympic champion

Further Reading

There is a wide range of books on different aspects of Austria.
Here are a few titles to start with.

Brook-Shepherd, Gordon. *The Austrians.*. London: Harper Collins, 1997.

Bousfield, Jonathan, and Rob Humphreys. *Austria, The Rough Guide.*
London/New York: 2005.

Czerniewicz-Umer, Teresa, Joanna Egert-Romanowskiej, and Janiny
Kumanieckiej. *Austria.* London/New York: Dorling Kindersley, Eyewitness
Travel Guides, 2006.

Davies, Norman. *A History of Europe.* Oxford/New York: Oxford University
Press, 1996.

McCagg, Jr., William O. *A History of Habsburg Jews, 1670–1918.*
Bloomington, Indiana: Indiana University Press, 1992.

Pynsent, Robert (ed.). *Decadence and Innovation: Austro-Hungarian Life
and Art at the Turn of the Century.* London: Weidenfeld and Nicolson,
1989.

Toman, Rolf (ed.). *Vienna: Art and Architecture.* Cologne, Germany:
Könemann, 1999.

Waissenberger, Robert (ed.). *Vienna in the Biedermeier Era, 1815–48.* New
York: Mallard Press, 1982.

Wheatcroft, Andrew. *The Habsburgs.* New York/London: Viking, 1995.

Williams, Geraint (ed.) *Time Out Vienna.* London: Ebury, 2005.

Austria, The Green Guide. Watford, U.K.: Michelin, 2001.

Fodor's German for Travelers (CD Package). New York: Living Language,
2005.

German. A Complete Course. New York: Living Language, 2005.

German Business Companion. The Language Guide for Business.
New York: Living Language, 1998.

In-Flight German. New York: Living Language, 2001.

Index

Acknowledgments

Special thanks for their support and patience to Alison, my wife, and Kate,
my daughter-in-law, as well as many friends in and from Austria.